This Scribe, My Hand

Works by Ben Belitt

Poetry

The Five-Fold Mesh

School of the Soldier

Wilderness Stair

The Enemy Joy: New and Selected Poems

Nowhere but Light

The Double Witness

Possessions: New and Selected Poems

Essays

Adam's Dream: A Preface to Translation

The Forgèd Feature: Toward a Poetics of Uncertainty

Translations

Four Poems by Rimbaud: The Problem of Translation

Federico García Lorca, *Poet in New York*

Selected Poems of Pablo Neruda

Antonio Machado, *Juan de Mairena* and *Poems from the Apocryphal Songbooks*

Selected Poems of Rafael Alberti

Pablo Neruda, A New Decade: Poems, 1958–1967

Pablo Neruda, *Poems from Canto General*

Rafael Alberti/Robert Motherwell, *To Painting*

Pablo Neruda, *Splendor and Death of Joachim Murieta* (play)

Pablo Neruda, *New Poems: 1968–1970*

Pablo Neruda, *Five Decades: Poems, 1925–1970*

Pablo Neruda, *Skystones*

Pablo Neruda: Late and Posthumous Poems

Selected works by Federico García Lorca, Eugenio Montale, Jorge Guillén, Jorge Luis Borges

This Scribe, My Hand

The Complete Poems of

Ben Belitt

Louisiana State University Press
Baton Rouge

1998

Manufactured in the United States of America
First printing

07 06 05 04 03 02 01 00 99 98 5 4 3 2 1

Designer: Amanda McDonald Scallan
Typeface: Bembo
Typesetter: Wilsted & Taylor Publishing Services
Printer and binder: Edwards Brothers, Inc.

Library of Congress Cataloging-in-Publication Data
Belitt, Ben, 1911–
This scribe, my hand : the complete poems of Ben Belitt.
p. cm.
ISBN 0-8071-2323-4 (cloth : alk. paper). — ISBN 0-8071-2324-2 (pbk. : alk. paper)
I. Title.
PS3503.E39A17 1998
811′.54—dc21 98-42512
CIP

The poems herein were earlier published in collections titled: *The Five-Fold Mesh* (Alfred A. Knopf, 1938), copyright © 1930, 1932, 1933, 1935, 1936, 1937, 1938 by Ben Belitt; *Wilderness Stair* (Grove Press, 1955), copyright © 1955 by Ben Belitt; *The Enemy Joy* (University of Chicago Press, 1964), copyright © 1964 by Ben Belitt; *Nowhere but Light* (University of Chicago Press, 1970), copyright © 1970 by Ben Belitt; *The Double Witness* (Princeton University Press, 1977), copyright © 1977 by Princeton University Press; and *Possessions* (David R. Godine, 1986), copyright © 1938, 1955, 1964, 1971, 1978, 1985 by Ben Belitt. An earlier version of *School of the Soldier* was published in the *Quarterly Review of Literature*, Volume V, Number 1 (1949).

The author wishes to thank the editors of the following journals, in whose pages some of these poems first appeared: *Bennington Review, Botteghe Oscure, Encounter* (London), *Georgia Review, Harper's Bazaar, Harper's Magazine, Modern Poetry Studies, Mundus Artium, The Nation, The New Republic, The New Yorker, Poetry, Poetry Review, Quarterly Review of Literature, Salmagundi, Silo, Sewanee Review, Southern Review, Virginia Quarterly Review, Yale Review.*

The author is grateful to the following foundations and for the following grants and awards, which allowed him to devote time and attention to the writing of many of the poems that appear in this volume: the Shelley Memorial Award, the Brandeis Creative Arts Award, the Chicago Civic Arts Award, the Guggenheim Foundation, the National Endowment for the Arts, the Russell Loines Award for Poetry of the American Academy and Institute of Arts and Letters, the Rockefeller Foundation Grant Bellagio (Italy), Yaddo Corporation, the University of Virginia, Bennington College.

This book was published with the assistance of a grant from the Norman and Rosita Winston Foundation.

The paper in this book meets the guidelines for permanence and durability of the Committee on Production Guidelines for Book Longevity of the Council on Library Resources. ♾

For Robert and Peggy Boyers

Contents

IV. The Enemy Joy (1955–1963)

I

POSSESSIONS

(1977–1990)

THOREAU ON PARAN CREEK

The freeze bears down
from this icy table-top in its mask of Kabuki
flour, and waits for the leavener's hand, in a locker of bread.

Who shall provide for the wilderness loaf and the wine
in the hour of watery depredation—
the wounded water flayed with its alternate aftermath,
freezing and burning, the pond's skin laid open
in the thermal feasts of the fish, a cicatrix
stitched by a blind thermometer in bandages of sleet,
a Gadarene dragonfly
drying its fleeces and zincs on the stone
that was given to strike and the water, to drink?

    Thoreau, with sounding line and chains,
    studied the bottom and dredged for an answer: *"Why*
    do precisely these objects make up a world?" he wrote
    in the salt of his thought,
    counting the bubbles, moving from cradle-hole and fault
    to the icy rosette at the center
    where Satan sat in the lobes and the glacial fat, hearing
    what Dante and Cotton Mather heard: the "diluvial crash"
    of the source, a booming of bees, and beyond,
    the breaking floe in the underground caves of the pond.

But nothing stands firm. Nothing keeps adamantine.
The water's block works downward
from opalescence, and the granite bores up
from a fiery hub that holds like the spokes of a wheel.
The solids sicken and mend, tangle
and loosen their lustre, hungry for metamorphosis.
The drowned demoniac sleeps in the lariat noose of the zero,
and Thoreau drifts in a berry-box.
                                His mind glistens,
disobedient, festive, a spinner.
                            He pays out his plummet.
He listens.

for Bernard Malamud

VOYAGE OF THE *BEAGLE*

If, as the poets say, life is a dream, I am sure in a voyage these are the visions which best serve to pass away the long night.

Love of the chase is an inherent delight in man.

—Charles Darwin

Hunting the old divinity of species
like Adam, he entered the peaceable kingdom
and saw at Galápagos a Chinese universe
supported by tortoises like an emperor's bibelot.

In his string-bag, over the chart tables, ear to the
ocean's floor, vomiting hardtack and gall,
he palpated the breathing of plates and the jostling
of continents, knowing nothing was finished—
Creation's sixth day, John's seven churches,
the conversions and the martyrdoms of Paul,
awaited their huntsman-interpreter—the bola's arc
flung from the fist of a Patagonian horseman
while the species still worked in the dark.

And gathered the delicate evidence on Alice's
tea table in a dream of enormity
diminishing into the infinitesimal: first,
the bleeding of marble and waterspouts,
the clouds of Magellan, the moving and shaking of birds,
the Malthusian savage computing his global migrations
in surds and quadratic equations, Friday's
footprint vanishing into the rainforest; then,
a "rattling of stones" at the surf line, the lace-
makers knotting the atolls with fungus and coral,
the locusts of Luzon, the flea:

till all was Edenic diversity. The animal
mystery opened the way to the thirteen
mutations of spiders and mice, the finches'
metamorphoses, seventy times seven, including
the species named Charles, the eternal turned into

the heterogeneous, the hunted lay down with the hunter.

And the beached hypochondriac, indoors with the bread and the wine
of his pharmacopoeia, opened a page of his journal.

for Fred Burkhardt

MARCH WILLOWS

This kindling of sacramental color—El Greco's
collapsed Count, a cadaver of haze, the green
of a closed or an opening grave,

fillets under the bent
wands, diagrams of fountains
rising and falling in faintly sinister gases,

phosphorus and pistachio—
yields to its seasonal summoner as the diamond
yields to the shock of the diamond-breaker's hammer.

Now the daft
ward of a mad song hacks at her laces
and spins in her farthingale's balloon

under the deckle of a mortuary tree
past Kedron and Babylon,
dangling her weeper's hair

and combing the primitive
leaf in valances and serrations—
a stonecutter's sense of the willow

chiseled in airy chartreuse.
O the mind breaks this way and that, says the summoner,
of its own crazed weight, shows an anvil's

underside, as the catamount's breath is seen
a moment between the thunderhead in the snow
and a glinting of evergreen,

while the whole of the willow breathes like a heart,
turning its ragbag of leaves
one way leaden, like the meat of an olive,

the other way, yellow, and the lute in the stone
is heard in its lunatic sweetness
in a rising and falling of branches:

O willow, willow!

SUMAC

I have seen
The incunabula of the divine grotesque.
—Hart Crane

1.

The incunabula of the malign
that bloodies a summer with no obvious intent
to harm, raising the sumac's fist

on a gargoyle of waxes and berries,
a coxcomb with its brickdust wattles
bared, like maggots swarming,

is yet to come. Today
the malice is gone from the sumac. The delicate
balances drop either side the stem,

conservative as a fern, pinnate
and symmetrical. Nightcrawlers, creels,
a litter of cardboard containers and tins, the fishpoles, the boys,

the nude child with his pocketed father
booted in rubber and smelling of woodsmoke and plaid,
unreel in a cavern of leaves. The grass

is flashing with fishheads. Under the lilac's rot
the marauders sniff an illicit aroma:
acne and marijuana. Sinkers bobble. The bells: it is Sunday.

2.

That year of the suicide, the creek
took the print of her wretchedness: a hummock
of laundry face-down in the sumac's thicket,

and burned with habitual daisies. My dream
of the Drum Room returned,
with its bonfire of rawhide and brasses, its

captain's insignia glowing alongside the drumsticks,
stacked sheet music, gold braid,
the boy in the hangar too late for the evening formation,

dazed in the Drum Captain's arms, watching the sleepy
parade, while the sticks whirred with primitive messages,
and under the tympanum's hoop,

the crossed cords on the drum,
the man's hand guided the child's to the sheltering place at the center
where the sumac opened its pouch in the leafy graffiti.

3.

All reads so easily now—the doorposts and plate glass of a
village with their initials and capital letters, a trout's
back seen through the gloss

of a sign-painter's fantasy. They say
all that is needed to say. "There's
the greengrocer's logo; there under the bar-lights,

The Villager's comic cartoon; a spaceman's balloon
in a glinting of newsprint; the spine
of a split book; the poem." They say what is common to all

and lives again in the noon
of the near and beholdable, as though nothing
could ever grow darker. Yet there

at the summit, in the sumac's
topmost corona, the cone of the summer cockade prepares
its swarthy declension again: feathers and spearheads

unscathed in a jungle of asterisks, pinpoints, suspension
dots—Lilliput's minuscule orchards written
on air in phosphor and punk with a Fourth of July sparkler.

4.

Why should I see you today in a pantry-door's
brass in the Orphanage kitchen?
Little sister, I was wiping the paste with a chamois under the platters

when suddenly you were there
with your gift of a breadcrust hidden away in your bloomers.
A bell shocked us awake. We stepped out on the steel

of a fire escape suspended together at three in the morning.
We looked down to the court where we dangled our legs
for a movie. You were

under the trees gathering pitch on the playground—
the green scum banding the bark for the midsummer
plague of caterpillars. You were pasting

cutouts in my copybook. We stared
through the Orphanage gates at a trophy of paper: *"Mother,*
come closer!" We waited. And *"Stay!"* we said. *"Stay!"* Then fifty
years later,

jailed in your fears, an offended spectator, she came
through the sumac, the reddening grass and ailanthus, to your cancerous
condominium window. A telephone rang you away.

5.

Which way to the sumac? The Indian tanners
are softening their leathers somewhere with its acids and chalks,
the bog-walkers, rooting for pitcher-plants, poison their shins

with its venoms. I remembered Chichén—the jade jaguar's heart flung
with the necklace of claws in a grain-god's *cenote,*
the Vesuvial bronzes and blacks of implacable fruitage—

all the warring mutations, benign or malignant by turns, that work in the
species, devising a wart knobbled over, a tumor, a pollen to steep
for the tea of a rabbit in waistcoats, a devil's caduceus:

mahogany, laurel, or sugarbush—which?
They say that Proserpine passed with her pomegranate through a column
of sumac to kindle her bloody flambeaux with its berries. Now

all the torches are lit in the atrium. The landscape is dangerous.
In the distance the gatherers go in their nightly guerrillas
mining the creeks of the village, in their broken

fatigues screened with leaves like chain lightning, intent
upon pillage. They wait where the roads and the bridgeheads begin.
Underneath, in the branches and pennants, the sumac's grenade is ready.

6.
The marauders move in. They lean toward the terrible fruitage, grope
for the ring in the carapace, feel how it bleeds to their bite
like the pith of the pomegranate, pierced.

They pull the pin.

WALKER

Death to the Lady said
While she to dancing measures still
Would move
—Léonie Adams

Stalled in a country house, in an angle of her walker,
her gaze, grown useless and exigent, holds a threshold,
a doorframe, a quadrant of Candlewood Mountain.

On the baize
background of her longing, a thought peaks and explodes,
vanishes in string-bags and pockets:

"Today I just had to go out for a walk—"

The world offers no loving concessions. In the peaceable
kingdom, blackberries aim their inks in an open portcullis,
armed with a cockerel's spurs.

"*—only as far as the clearing,*" she thinks.

The V of her walker descends and descends.
She has left
the interior world of staircases, rag rug, quotidian
obstacle races. Matted with accident, she flattens the weedy
largesse of her passing and levels the meadow in wedges.

"Those are the mowers of Marvell," she says. "Those,
the child's valedictions, an autumnal acrostic of
leaves. I remember the violet-gatherers, the horns and the hares
of a festival, the runners with lots, the gleaners, the sowers,
the sheaves. And those are the grapes and the shears."

Uncaring, the summer's exuberance breaks like a surf on her
passage. She veers in the salt and contingency, spinning an invisible
mariner's wheel, a figurehead rising and falling in chicory: rides
over the paddles and flails of a threshing floor, last looks and
dismemberings, flaws in a lost cornucopia.

The vise of her walker
is blossoming.

"I see brackets of grapeleaves," she says, "a sundial's
planchette and a whimsical compass's point spelling out
messages, thunderheads printing the air. . . . "
a dancer, prosthetic in iron, gasping with steam on the
cloth, measuring time for the dithyramb and moving the chorus.

"I have come to dance out the quarrier's joy on the flint
of an age's abandonment."
The gods in the walking-machine
beckon to her from the clearing.
She enters the ring of the dancers.
She is theirs.

ANNUNCIATION TO JOSEPH

Looking up from the bole
on the ringleted carpenter's block,
the incense under the saw,
he paused as the blade buckled and the sunburst
opened an improbable fan in its blinding serrations.

And thought:
                    All goes as it must.
A fragrance of resin and camphor sweetens the sawhorse.
The ruler's edge measures the place where the stylus
passed over, to a decimal fraction,
the part vanishes into the whole, wedge matches wedge
and confirms the plumb line's vibration.
The reckoning is just.

Then how is it everything goes so abstract?
The blueprint trembles with musical signatures,
and wherever the balancing bubble has lain
an angel works in the grain,
the posts of the temple are moved (as the prophet has said)
and the saw's tooth snaps on the knot.

What should a sawyer's apprentice
know of the marvelous, or an angel require
of him? One beam weighs down another.
The roof rises over the inn and the stable,
the pedestal leaps from the plinth.
Shall the thing that is building rise on a palpable loss?
The journeyman has his reward, the builder is worthy his hire.

I am moved by no journeyman thing.
I smell dung on the terebinth
floor, and the ox's stall curves like a cradle.
The arches reject the seams of the pillar in their
Roman similitude and
pull to a point, as if to outdistance creation
and gather all under their wing.

Something is building.
The consort of Solomon calls from the garden:
the godson awakes with the bridegroom
and the virgin lies down with the bride.
Shall they join what the axe and the hammer never hewed
out of cedar and granite?
Does the whole of the carpenter's subtlety end and begin
with a cross?

A carpenter's son does well to be wary.
Hail, Mary!

POSSESSIONS

for Nick Mayer

1.

The shameful last shovelful
that forced the burial doors
on all that pharaonic junk: a boy-king's rumpus room
of funerary boats, inlays of faience and ebony
for a fowler's boomerang, long-necked amphorae,
wig boxes, gold-leaf pectorals, dismantled chariot wheels—
the toy-rooms of Tutankhamen—

and there under his three sarcophagi,
the dispossessed possessor in his headstrong barricade,
no longer Nilus's god, but a violated
child, cross-armed and disemboweled, stockpiled in the silt,
his abdomen scoured with palm wine, myrrh, papyrus,
his cheekbone carven with spices and verdigris,
holding the flail and the crook of the Heliopolitan
under a top-heavy crown, his eyes like ankhs
in the gilt and lapis lazuli, staring the tomb-robbers down.

2.

"I waked to my perishing things,
ownerless and provisional, in a field of bric-a-brac.
I heard the tumblers yield
to a safecracker's fingertips while the despoilers
took possession, crowding the Theban desert
with turquoise and chalcedony, pendants, gold falcon-heads,
baboons—
all the inviolable iconography of transcendence:

" 'Mother,' I said, 'Mother:
I thought to come with my footstool and abacus
as in the nonage of my schooldays, whistling for Anubis.
It is frightening to wake in a windowless broom-closet
of a crypt where even my playthings turn into menacing attributes
and cutthroats and curators covet my souvenirs from Memphis.
Where is the godhead safe, if not at the pyramid's point—

Osiris's honeycomb
sealed by the goldsmith and caulked with shipmaker's resin?
What do we bring to the gods if not corn from the banqueter's
table,
linens from Karnak, the artifacts and baggage of our status?
If nothing has followed us there, if
nothing has stirred in the desert but some nondescript intruder,
if an Englishman from Cairo with a writ for our arrest
lays violent hands on a Pharaoh's portion, after the long hiatus—
if nothing is ever reborn,
what have we ever possessed?' "

3.
Midwinter in the Firehouse. The Creek prints
its double parchment in the icy splinter-play: the upper
scroll of the Falls on the bottommost scroll of the Falls:
a midrash of hieroglyphs.

A fortress's thickness divides
the furnace-room from the freeze on the other side of the wall.

In the cellar's glacial cement
I breathe in the gas of the dehumidifier,
count calories in the knocking of the furnace, dream semiotic
pageants, trace fractions of oil on the arrowhead of the gauges. I stash
what I can in the vanishing sound of the bells.
I ready the trash.
Overhead, at the peak of the roof—
the pyramid's point where the architect carved from the block
a sundeck for a tentative sun-worshiper—I hear the tomb-robber's
hammer tap at my crypt of books. I count my Egyptian
possessions:
Alberti's angels and doves in the pane of a coffee-table;
Lorca, Neruda, Siqueiros; Motherwell cutting acidulous prisms
in metals and piercing the walls with a pope's fenestrations;
Rocky, my Firehouse familiar, with a pugilist's paws and panache;
some chimerical keepsakes a tourist might filch from a flea market—
glass paperweights, millefleurs, or a dandelion's pinwheel in plastic;

sarapes; some Mexican gesso; Chac Mool
recumbent, looking over his shoulder toward Uxmal
or Palenque; a Peruvian drummer in whimsical candy-stripes; my
steel file of duplicate documents—all the rubbish
of Thoth and Tutankhamen, with that glint of the private
and poignant—Andromeda held in the loop of the void like a zodiac:
a collector's vagaries metamorphosed into possessions
I would heap at the door if I could, to interpret
my lost predilections and repeat my identity.

Nicky and Judy and Eddy and Robert and Dusty—
deliver my things from the vandals!

The Creek jostles its darknesses under the ice.
Below is a roaring, a grating of angles and edges, a slobber,
a drowning.
The boiler-room readies its column of blood in the shaken
thermometer and sets forth on the torrent.

What have we ever possessed?
I wait for the tomb-robbers.

THIS ROCK

The rock, in the salt meander,
the bison-back nuzzling the sea-holly
in a drench of coppery bubbles, chain mail, saliva,
repeating a sponge's disguises,
speaks for the animal mystery.

It puzzles like scrimshaw,
whittling its bulk to a mote for the
pouch of a slingshot. It works in the watery waste
where the particles enter,
calls us to dance with Democritus,

and points to the plummeting
center. Below, in the lair of the
octopus, Peter quarries his drowning cathedral, the polyp
readies its gargoyles and waterspouts,
pools gather like isinglass,

Leviathan basks by the reefs,
plane over plane in the plankton,
confounding the Comforters, reflecting, reversing, refining,
turning substance to essence, being to immanence,
basalt and mica to ether:

and above, in the void of that other
Beginning, floats the stone that we
read by, the mariner's or the sybil's, that mimics the tides and
the solstice and casts back the parched
and nocturnal in its freezing redundance—

the moon of the gypsy diviner
who measures by crescents and quadrants, writes
in cartographer's chalks in the desert where the astronaut's boot,
the whips of the punishing Pharaohs,
the charioteers, all splinter at last.

BRUTTO TEMPO: BELLAGIO
(Lake Como)

for Gina Werfel

The eye and its alpenstock cannot force their way
back to the passes—that tiara of peaks for a storm-king, stainless
steel on majolica moist from the artisan's

brushstroke. Today, all is the mash
of a hack's mistranslation: terza rima, chiaroscuro,
gravure on the slopes, roof-tiles in a hachure

of cloudy serrations like a tortoise's armature or the
underside of a shell, a rotting away
of the pear blossoms, implacable ash and decay—

all the forfeits of outline, dimension, enclosure,
a perspective of circles and cycles for a Dantean parable,
a purgatorial heath for Doré.

Nothing remains of the Village: only pockets
in packets, cauldrons and fissures, as though
a lake smoldered and broke in the fog

in a rubbish of cypress and ochre. Yet
below, the boats still stand unscathed in the scatter—spent wicks
in a spindle of hurricane glass,

in the pewter and tin of the coves. In the workshops of Como
silk boils on the looms like milkweed and dandelion
seed. Demogorgon has breathed

on the glass. The volatile life
of the imminent—self-loss and self-manifestation—
wrestle like opposite presences,

thigh to thigh, for the gift of a blessing. But here
in the pit, nothing prodigious
acknowledges the workings of providence. There is

only Gina, come down from the Villa,
her outrageous umbrella striped like a medicine ball
for the balancing act of a poodle,

to toil in the clottings of fog and the world's
suppuration, bearing her paint box, a scrap of stretched
canvas, an improbable easel—a vulnerable

mote in the wind and the void. Her brush's point churns
in a plasm of oil, ascending, descending,
preparing a lane to the passes

till the wet of the canvas is covered and the color is total.
Peak after peak reassembles. Her alpenstock strikes for
the palette's horizon and holds firm on the glazes

and she waves back to us from the summit.

ESMISS ESMOOR*

God si love

Having no thumb for navigational cunning,
no wish to shore up a bowsprit with the blind eye
and décolletage of a figurehead, I am
reduced to this: a tripper, aging in cardigan,
nursing a pittance of beef broth for its moment of
warmth, decked on the leeward side, sailing for England.

A needle works in the shrouds and my
deck chair yaws like a spinnaker.

I go voyaging
over caverns and courtrooms and mosques, spelunker
of nightmares and marriages, while a voice
in the void thrashes and settles without echo or issue—
bo-oum and *bo-oum* and *bo-oum*—in a
troglodyte's language.

For a moment,
all sways like the fan of a punkah. A gavel
smashes on teak, like a battle-mace.

It is the
picnic in Marabar again—a rapist's excursion
to a jungle of Indian courtesies and juridical
voices, or a god's day of overturned boats,
fetuses drowning in semen, nausea, depression. All
spins in an ocelot's widening eye, and grows feral.
I step from the sponge and the cloth of my sandals
and a young man repeats his Mohammedan formula:
You are one of us!, bowing in crumpled madras.

One of us? One of us? *What should I know*
of the Ninety-Nine Attributes?

*Mrs. Moore, disavowing all loyalties and divinized by her admirers as "Esmiss Esmoor," turns her back on the compounding disasters of her visit to India, and dies en route to England, having accomplished nothing.

I faint
in the mangroves and toddy palms. I claw in the dark of the cave.
I ready the flint and the straw for a matriarch's
sacrifice. My own get torments me. I lessen and lessen
in a world of subalterns. I am naphtha, nothingness,
carrion. I quail in the fetor of rank
copulation, see sweat on a triangle furred like
a bat, the Solomon's seal on the pubis of Priapus,
the horse of Apocalypse baring a uvula
scorched by a planet's explosion:

bo-oum and *bo-oum* and *bo-oum* . . .

My broth goes to vinegar. No one will lift
a beneficent finger to steady the suppliant's cup
or beckon me back to my father's verandah.
The fan will not yield to the weight of the winnower.
There is nothing to breathe on the bay.

Yet I sail
toward the son of the blessing as though all were made one
in retributive havoc and innocence: the sea-lanes
to England, and the pestilent ash of the Ganges.

Heartbeat by heartbeat, I emerge from the cave
of libidinous taint on the quick of my footsoles,
empty of being.

Buddha laughs from the Bo Tree of Gya,
and behind him, the night-hag, the umbilical boy, and the saint.

A wasp stitches his way through the mandala,
writing all down with the sexual bone of his stinger.

The air smells of honey and gossamer.

The web widens from ocean to ocean.

homage to E. M. Forster

GRAFFITI

Till all was in readiness:

There, in my vandal's dream,
the straphangers sagged under the lictor's festoon
of their nooses, and the coaches bored through the tinder.

The sound was a jackhammer's sound, the sizzle
of flanges and bits in a gun barrel. The light was peacock blue—
blue as the tossing of flares in a troughing of water or
the glinting of spice in a urinal, blue as the night-light
in a crescent of vanishing corridors—cornflower
and chicory blue on the standing tooth of vermilion
that strikes the sum of the burning.
Spray-gun in hand,
in the tomb-robber's darkness, I dreamed of my double
initials: a jungle liana of loops in a gangster's cartouche, a beanstalk
of curlicues, calligrams, cave scribbles branching flintily out
to the roof like the smoke from a pistol.
I tasted the charge
of the rails to the roots of my nostrils, and the tunnels erupted
in a hashish explosion.

There were the platforms
and carriages, the time-lapse ascents of the pods for a giant
branching over and under: the reds and the greens of a tapeworm
cartography stinting the windows with a knifegrinder's
emery hiss, the guillotines venting their closures and
human discharges, the placenames, the stations . . .

So I struck with the
felt of my marker. I struck. I struck at the windows. I struck
under the bulbs through the flying chromes and aluminum
with the mark of my lifetime's rejections till all
turned to neon.

There was my name with its starving
imprimatur. All glowed with my signature—
the studs of the girders, the crossties, the gritty enamels,

the sheath on the heart of the diesels.
It said
B over B over B over B over B, in the code
of a banker's equivalence.

"You know me," I wrote with my spray-gun.
"You know me, you mandarin wards of the bitch-goddess,
gatekeepers there at the change-boxes, flashing your semaphores:

'This far and no further! He gets only as far
as the spokes of the turnstile! Close off the exits,
the fireman's poles to the kiosks,
the pornographer's heaven of nipples
and penises!
The subject is armed and dangerous!'"

But already the walls blazed with
bison and horn. My downstrokes and capital
letters were scored into room after room of the coven, slashed
with the inks of my underground rages, the singular vowel
of my losses.
It said
I it said I it said I it said I.

That way,
I thought, it could be done. That way
my vengeance could work in the manholes, Jocanaan's vow
could carry my manifestations to the barns at the end of the run.
Never mind the comings and goings two stories above
in the streets! Never mind the nightsticks and badges,
the comedy chase of the transit police!

That way, the signs
could be carved into the domes of the blinded macadam,
the caravans, seared with my brand, drink deep at the railyards in the iron
savannahs, the Alexandrian libraries rearise from the flames
and the whole of the canon be one.

CROSSING THE ICE: ACAPULCO

The children are flying,
non-poisonous,
tentacular, in bladders
and blisters of nylon, Mary Poppins umbrellas,
over a groundglass Pacific, dangling
amphibian thighs as though weighing the thread
of their altitude
in the pans of their testicles.

Below,
the tours gather sunburn and coconut oil, bubble like
squids from the lobbies and discotheques, clot
and decaffeinate on the boomerang
curve of the shorefronts.

Tamed to a diver's
cliché, hazard rehearses its gig
on the cliffs. Flea markets jostle
the swarming costeras. A pony barouche coasts in its harness
of colored balloons.

It is time for the toucans, the mechanical sewer rats,
T-shirts inscribed with the last metamorphic declensions
of Ovid, a daiquiri slush
of erotica feathered with green and magenta.

It was hard
to live under an icicle's point with a snowblower's rectitude,
freeze to a halt and tunnel a lane from Vermont
to this Walden for surfeiters.

Now the horsemen of Cortés
debouch on a fairway of chicklets. The mendicant mothers
sleep sound in a midnight of sandals.

Under
a sunset's tortilla
I balance my way home to my perils
on a black-and-white ice-cake, with Eliza and Lillian.

THE BATHERS: A TRIPTYCH

The moving waters at their priestlike task
Of pure ablution round earth's human shores.
—John Keats

1. *Marat's Assassination* (David)
In the tub, with Marat, in the steam of the
overturned pitchers, the painter prepared
his toilette for a doomed neurasthenic—

disinfectants and balms for a scrofulous
zealot and the itch of his body-sores,
encaustics to swaddle his lesions: marinations,

emollients: Job in a sitzbad,
dipping the nib of his quill in the optics of Newton,
the bloodbaths of Necker and Danton, in a

turban of surgical gauzes, thinning his line
to the width of a suture's impasto, draining the colors
and crushing the sponges

and signing his nakedness
with a killer's stiletto, till nothing was left
but a blazon

of bathing and bandages, and the finical
signature: "This is my discourse on light, my hemorrhage
written in sizing and soap bubbles: JACQUES LOUIS DAVID."

2. *The Swimming Hole* (Eakins)
Doubtless, the abandoned palette, with its thumb-hole
for the reconnoitering hand that held the colors up,
lies just where the painter left it

on a holiday impulse—a hand's span
outside the frame that walls his picture in
and inundates his easel.   Nakedness

has made the painter one with his
subject and the paint that he
swims in: nothing

can keep the Philadelphian
apart from his subject in the bath of the
pigment's wash; painter and swimmer

dive and resurface together, look back at their
double immersion with a floater's naked intent,
laying on color and building two triangles of men

like a saltimbanque, till a drowned world lives
in the brush's saturation, and a minimal
Adam emerges in a strobe-light's sequences:

first, the reclining figure, left,
yielding forearm and flank to the whimsical masonry; then,
the beckoning and the receding ones, baring

a buttock's valentine
or balancing an arm; then, the diver
in his headlong belly whopper;

and above, on the plinth of the canvas,
full-figure, the vulnerable contemplator, midway between
a slouch and a straddle, arms akimbo, dreaming

a skinny-dipper's readiness to plunge, equally at home
in the paint that is water's oblivion,
and the water that is one with the paint.

3. *Woman Bathing* (Degas)
An end to laundry, then. The yawning *lavandière*
tries the patina of her flatiron with a bubble
of spittle, and the sempstress

stabs her milliner's pin into a nosegay of
ribbons and wicker. The absinthe-drinkers, the ballerina
benched by the blackened duenna and her

folded umbrella, kneading a knotted
Achilles tendon in the total conflagration
of the theater's ensemble—

vendettas, tutus, semaphores of shoulders
and refracted scintillations, harems
of the half-worlds of Montmartre,

bitten into metal or streaked with wet pastel: all
stand to the brimming circuit of a basin's tin,
disrobe, at the painter's bidding, and disclose

a geometer's parabola of Lilith and Susannah,
while the watcher in the reeds,
the mad old king who shipwrecked on the barrens,

feels the replenishing pity of his nakedness
again, puts on drapery and word, presence and essence
again, and the rites of ablution are done.

LILY BRISCOE: A FAILED PAINTING

Even the painters on frost, the breakers
of mazes and mandalas who are given to know,
tell us: *"All givens are unknowns."*

What if
the sizing blinds them, at first, and they flinch—still the
brush perseveres, color opens a grid in the canvas's brine, and
suddenly, the mine in the pith of the prism is there:

the spearhead of a mournful countenance, or a
chamberpot on a haunted head under a windmill's paddle,
a clown's sudarium—contingency's overplus: all
gathers, sweatdrop by sweatdrop, in the canvas's rainforest—

then the hand withdraws from the palette
and the picture fails.

But suppose all that is given is failure, dishevelment, vertigo—
a thirsty Lighthouse's beacon awaiting foul weather,
a masochist father's negation, denying
the child's pledge of a picnicker's tomorrow,
Mrs. Ramsay by her window,
wasted with mercy, dying in parentheses,
with nothing given, or forgiven, or forgotten—

suppose
that much is known to us, that much is given—

and suppose that a Sunday
painter, watching a boatload of malcontents grope toward a joyless
horizon—some spinster, landlocked, uncertain of the crossing,
should measure the Lighthouse's distance with a paintbrush's
faltering inches, find the point of return and mark down
the darknesses with a lucky slashing of pigments—

moving a tree from the foreground to the canvas's middle
perspective, and fixing it there—

some
amateur of providence or bereavement, crying from the heart
to an absent reader of hearts:

"Mrs. Ramsay! Mrs. Ramsay! Mrs. Ramsay!"

—and lay down her brushes in extreme fatigue
and say: *"It is finished. . . . "*

Would the known
be given, at last, and the given be there?

homage to Virginia Woolf

DISPLACED PERSON

The history of deprival, with its dowser's bounty
of forfeitures, self-loss, parricidal
mornings on Moriah, its slaughterer's
knife stropped for the child of promise
and the surrogate beast pinned to the pyx of the thicket,
speak for our wintry displacements.
We barter
a habit's terrain for the solstice's shock
of reversal, ready the faggots
on a glacier's untimely crevasse, come with our
seasonal longing to challenge the Genius of Place
and repeat some remembered return, as though all
were restorable.

All to no purpose.
The vanished epiphany shows no backward sweep
of the needle, no ratchet's division of numerals
on the dial of our banishment, no mandate
to give back our heart's divination.

All at once, our landscapes disown us: the thunderhead
on Sangre de Cristo, riding its hard little anvil
ten thousand feet over Taos or Santo Domingo,
billowing gases and venoms at two o'clock in the afternoon,

discharges its ampere of rain with no thought
for the fragile observer. The transparency over the Gorge,
plumed Quetzalcoatl ablaze on his swastika,
forces his arrowhead in sunbursts of maize
and magenta. The Cuban poinsettia, starring
a swathe of tobacco on the Key West horizon,
blackens the antic banana.

But the voyage is elsewhere.
Elsewhere
the bush burns, and the desert warns with its voices:

"Draw not nigh hither, put off thy shoes
from thy feet, for the place where thou standest
is nowhere, and suffers no human return
Yours was a vagrant's eidolon, a Bedouin's mirage
that was never a portion of destiny: the passing
connivance of joy. Burning in Carthage,
the saint barters all for a figment
of memory, enters the fiery garden of his
pagan beatitude, and reads under the heavy
forefinger of Monica: 'Place there is none.
We go backward and forward and there is no place.
Tolle lege!
              Take up the book.
                              Empty the pages.
                                        Read on!' "

II

THE DOUBLE WITNESS

(1970–1976)

. . . this want of witness in brute nature . . .

—Gerard Manley Hopkins
Letter to W. R. Dixon

. . . reckon but, reck but, mind
But these two; ware of a world where but these two tell, each
off the other.

—Gerard Manley Hopkins
"Spelt from Sibyl's Leaves"

XEROX

The original man lies down to be copied
face down on glass. He thinks what it is
to be other than he was, while the pilot light
goes garnet, a salamander's eye
blinks in the camera's cave, green burns like the skin
of the water seen by a surfacing swimmer:
and the moving and shaking begin.

What must it be, to be many? thinks the singular
man. Underneath, in the banked fluorescence, the rollers
are ready. A tarpaulin falls. A humming of flanges
arises, a sound like rail meeting rail
when power slams out of the fuses. A wick explodes
in the gases—and under the whole of his length
the eye of the holocaust passes.

And all that was lonely, essential, unique
as a fingerprint, is doubled. Substance and essence,
the mirror and the figure that printed the mirror,
the deluge that blackened creation and the hovering pigeon
with the leaf's taste in its beak,
are joined. The indivisible sleeper is troubled:
What does it mean to be legion?

he cries in the hell of the copied. The rapists, the lovers,
the stealers of blessings, the corrupt and derivative
devils, whirl over the vacant emulsion.
The comedian peers from the brink and unsteadily copies
its laughter. The agonist prints its convulsion.
Like turns to like, while the seminal man on the glass
stares at his semblance and calls from the pit of the ink:

Forgive our duplicity. We are human
and heterogeneous. Give us our imitations!
Heart copies heart with a valentine's
arrows and laces. The Athenian dream and the adulterers paired
in the storm tell us the mirrors are misted. The whole of our art
is to double our witness, and wait. And the original man on the plate
stands and steps down, unassisted.

KITES: ARS POETICA

The innocents have come to make their cast
in the sky, fishing upside down
and flying heraldic signs, Chinese
or Euclidean, with parallel squares
and dotted balsam lines
in vanishing tissue paper—
heart-shapes, shields,
or whatever their breath
can bend to a crossbow of twine
or cut in armorial fields
and make fly—

like that other caster of lightning
paying out bamboo, watching the reel and the spinner
break electrical water,
touch a key in the creel
and blaze for the Philadelphian
with the shock of the trout's phosphorescence—

till, somewhere between the helicopter's star
and a vanishing point in the sea,
I feel myself go up,
unreeling aerial rigging out of my side
and shedding a helix of thread,

an invisible top in the air,
a spider climbing the light—
till the whole web bells and goes tight—
and I am flown by the kite.

SWAN LAKE

The swan, a stylist, born to the posture of a question mark
and the bishop's mitre—
balletic, episcopal, unsentimental,
a hater of Tchaikovsky, inadvertently
settling his calm posterior like a tutu, fixing his seedy
eyeball like a lorgnette in the garbage and crumbs—
is nobody's accompanist. He leads
a hard flotilla in half a V,
parting the cattails, makes a fist
of his breastbone, aims the carroty wax of his beak,
and smashes the flat of the pond
till nothing is seen in the scum
but the double hose and albino spur of his rump.

Never having read
Ovid's *Metamorphoses,* he is content
with the basic changes of the uxorious loner:
his cygnets making chevrons in the swamp,
training for puberty, drifting like crumpled carbon paper
with the letters showing faintly through the smudge,
pica on *elite,*
till white burns through the hump
and all that was ordinary turns exceptional.

The swan is unreflective, opposing the hard outline
to the blur,
casting a classical image like the Parthenon
in an Ionian ambiguity of pomp,
oblivious to imagery, equivalent
only to itself. Those who have known his anger,
know the alternate side of a coin: tenderness
and homicidal hate—
the beer-drinking family man and the fighter
cocked with a trigger's violence,
showing the naked triangle of his uvula
parted to the gullet under a bony bulb, like the Guernica horses—

as the whole contrivance hisses and advances,
saying:
          Bastards! Bastards! Bastards!

                                        And tacks round
and stands its ground.

THE REPELLANT

for Melissa Hayden

Coming to dinner with the ballerina, in that improbable
weather of swans and necromancers, hunters
of holocaustal birds, scenarios in Ukrainian
magenta, we climbed the spas and stables,
rose in the yeasty heat of Saratoga,
found the place appointed in the fable—a
crossbow in a coronet of feathers—
and entered the open circle of the dancers.

Behind us, on the nether levels, blind
guests to the symposium of summer
sped on their simultaneous errands—the centaur's
stations in a universe of horses
stretching their charmed necks in a jockey's
collar of roses; Hassidim in bicarbonated water
singing in mineral gases, Victorian gingerbread,
Norwegian spruces, pizzas, Goldberg variations.

And then: the dancer's house, with its aquarian
windows clearing the trees' scrim, its birdbath
stance and unemphatic lawns, its pathway
like a tutu of begonias and nasturtiums; and
parallel to the sky, five candles of ultraviolet
repellant, cold cartridges of phosphorescent neon, traps
of mercurial darknesses and lights, magnetic
fields subtle with mosquitoes come to dance.

We talked, over the meat and flowers, while a darkening
world emptied the picture windows and blackened the colors,
dividing outer and inner, the propitious and the evil.
Only a blank pane, and the pathos of our
human conversation—breakable, incessant, overeager—
defined our dances from the dance of the mosquitoes:
the intriguer's infinitesimal banquets of blood,
from the love-feasts of a night's improvisations.

Beyond, in the starlit vault, the stingers swarmed,
ringing the candles in the revels of Oberon,
building quasars for the firebird and the swan,
pylons of acid and ink colored like
the venom in the jellyfish's blister,
the incendiary's gentian violet,
zodiacs of peacock-oils and pinks,
attracting and repelling, leading the dancers on,

as the whole house trembled in the dice-cup of a gambler.
The mosquitoes arched their backs on the sleeping village
and entered the burning nimbus, winding and unwinding
their skeins. The Prince of Darkness moved through the
Athenian wood, calling the flowers by name: *Pease-Blossom,*
Oxslip, Mustard-Seed. And the Pythoness
blazing with lice, at the spindle of creation,
smiled at her creaturely void, watching the colors dwindle.

And spat into the cinders.

DOUBLE POEM OF THE WORLD'S BURNING

1. *"Ah, Sunflower!"*

Preparing for that presence, the pod
chose a man's height, set its cleats in the leaves
like a steeplejack, scribbled its target of ovals,
and rose to eye level.

Climbing a profile of gardens, a Nimzo-Indian
chessboard of vegetables, villages, rock with its pollen
of lichen, the sunflower steadied its petals in zodiacal
yellow, and struck like a clock.

All the world's plenty, all the brazen particulars—a bull's-eye
of seeds with the pips pointing down into chain-metal, an obsidian
disk bulging with roe like a carp—took on the hardness
of Chinese enamels

and opened its perfect meniscus. Then the terrible
heaviness began—the failing of bronzes, the hasp at the sunflower's
center breaking away, a fading of planets, eclipses, coronas,
the falling and falling away of the petals—

Time's total weariness, the terrible weight in the sun—all
that hammers at darkness and glows like the baize of the table Van Gogh
saw at Arles, in the cornfields and candles: a madman painting the night
 till
the sky was delivered again to the crows.

2. *Glare: Atlacomulco*

And his raiment was white as the light.

The invisible life that sleeps in the grossness of things
and feeds on the bulk of the world
bringing substance and weight and degree—

the tumescence
that traces a thread in the loins, to the swamp
of our human duration

and insists on the blood and the bone of our presence—
shows the world's burning,
turned low, like the flame in the bell of the lamp.

Blue as acetylene, it waits
at the furthest edge of the morning, a transparency
holding a bird and a steely horizon:

the water repeats it: gunmetal on pewter,
pewter on ultramarine,
doubling the universe, spilling the colors

and shapes of a season
on the rubble and flint of a planet, crowding
the leaf to its uttermost margin, filling the spaces,

till nothing is latent, nothing withheld or unnameable:
the spike of the cactus, the fuse in the tulipan, the sun
at its zenith, lie flat on the plane of the sky like an armorer's anvil,

and the fullness of time is complete. Then
that burning away of the air, as the glowing erasure
of limit begins: a glare

on the claws and the cusps of poinsettia
tracing the heat's line with a solderer's iron, petal for petal—
a talon of ash

on a talon of smoking vermilion, forcing the fire at the center
to bloom on the edges and smolder like metal,
scoring the water

with hurrying scallops cut into friezes and crystals,
blowing the coal of the world's
calefaction till the unbinding of matter is done,

the visible turns into the invisible,
the invisible, into an omen, and out of the hearthbed of summer
the suffering hedonist stands forth—

the Man who came eating and drinking, whose clothing was white
as the light,
lifting his skull's lamp to the darkness and saying: *I am the Light
of the world!*—to deliver himself to the Romans.

THE GUANAJUATO MUMMIES

The body of those deaths is given us now (the child
guide says, for a peso) by a trick of mineral gases—the stale
exhalation of silver and the weight of the quarries—
with a potter's underground skills. In the cupboard's glass
plate stacking the corridor, the re-arisen
recumbents, clown-white on their jawbones, disgorging
a petrified vomit, are erect now.
                                        Parodists
of perpetuity in oversized jackets, with their funeral
pants at their ankles, top-bananas with corn-
kernel teeth and tarantular breastbones; their colors,
paraffin, gesso, parched brain-coral, adobe; their
attitudes, prudery, venery, impenitence;
their posture, forensic; fingers
folded under, like the wingbones of bats, da Vinci
flying machines; a spider's remainder of hair; the
pupils discernible under their oval cocoons;
their sex, a fold in pastry, slingshots, rosettes; some
raised to a toe-point, sinews locking like
cloves into garlic, baroque or balletic, others
driving the total weight of their dying into their sandals;
osso bucco and tin in the shanks; rib cages
like empty prosceniums, burnt estuaries, smashed cradles—
children of cheesecloth and candles, Noh-devils
fetal again in their death chambers of iron and chalk.

None will be naked again.
                                        The covert
and promiscuous life of the newly unburied, the
flamboyance their breathing concealed or their body's
avidity made poignant and virginal—fountains of
semen and spittle, penetrations, erections—we know
now, were a gift of the spirit, expenses of grace and election.
Robbed of their nakedness, the dead are robbed of their mystery.
In their bellies' overturned sacks a feral pornographer
fingers a testicle, nipples and wombs turn
sterile: chewed-paper wasp nests, winter apples, prunes.

Yet it is in their mouth that they speak to us still. The shock
of encounter with—what? a collapse of the will? the preposterous?
nothingness? the terminal truths of betrayal?—
has opened their jawbones like grackles, sprung all the hinges,
turned all the lips heart-shaped: wolf-whistles, the coloratura's
invisible shout that splinters the wineglass, the leer
of a gargoyle's bravura.

Inside the cage there is screaming.

The buried, the gassed, the self-murdered, the
pregnant, burn in the ovens of Auschwitz, kindle and crackle
like napalm in a blind conflagration of noises
pitched out of range like the ears of a pointing retriever:
crying havoc, vendetta, universal rejection, universal derision,
the rage of the charlatan saint and the faulted believer.

We come out into sunlight at last.

We see cut watermelons,
papaya, pyramidal oranges, gelatinous diamonds
where the pineapple sweetens its center in the hive's core.
We are wracked with the pangs of our fasting.

We are alive.
The children approach us with sugary ribbons:
"A mummy, señor?" And they offer us candy.

Mocking, solicitous, the children insist. The children wait to be paid.

We bite through the skulls in the cellophane wrappers.

We burn in the sunlight, afraid.

AN ORANGE IN MÉRIDA

The orange-peelers of Mérida, in the wrought-
iron midday, come with mechanical skewers
and live oranges, to straddle the paths
on caissons of bicycle wheels
and work in the dark of the plaza, like jewelers' cloths.

The orange is ceremonious. Its sleep
is Egyptian. Its golden umbilicus
waits in pyramidal light, swath over swath, outwitting
the Caesars. It cannot be ravaged by knives,
but clasps its mortality in, like the skein of an asp.

The bandstand glitters like bone, in laurel
and spittle. Behind their triangular
catafalques, the orange-peelers move through the thirst
of the world with Rameses' bounty
caulked into the hive of the peel

while ratchets and wheels spin a blazing
cosmology on their little machines. Under
skewers and handles, the orange's skin
is pierced, the orange, in chain-mail and papyrus,
unwinds the graveclothes of Pharaoh

in a helix of ribbon, unflawed, from the navel's
knot to the rind and the pulp underneath, like a butterfly's
chrysalis. And sleeper by sleeper, the living turn with their thirst
to each other, the orange's pith is broken
in a blind effervescence that perfumes the palate and burns

to the tooth's bite.
And the dead reawaken.

FROM THE FIREHOUSE*

for Paul Feeley

1. *From the Firehouse*

Living between two fires and two falls—a stairway
of watery risers and treads above and below, holding
the fish to its floor and the foam to the swallow's
intaglio, an old Firehouse and a new—I think only
of canvas, like a Bedouin. Now in the whimsical
playground of your cellar, that birthday-box of aerial toys,
beginning with the color red, as children do,
I listen for the engines folding their ladders in a burst
of exploding bells, a village in its underdrawers
wakened by the color red from its dream of sexual famine:
colors that bound from the canvas like a rubber ball
in a rite of counted jack-rocks, Cyclopean maces, panels
and chess pawns—your Euclidean signature, Paul.

And all night I hear a skip-rope slapping canvas
between the crated sculpture and the mildewing gravel
where your boxer-father dances, shedding the color red,
lashing a corner of the Engine Room with his dream of travel
that flings you toward the Spanish littoral and flings
you back, shedding the color red, mortal Moroccan red.

I build a house as you would build in cards or canvas,
with a gambler's riffle of whiskey and aces in spades,
or as your Damascan namesake built with a tent of
flames and sizing dazzled with lights and voices,
thumb to the palette like a bowling ball, breaking a string
of shapes and reassembling the shapes in identical frames
to demolish the spaces.

Trout-hunter, dawdling in feathers
and flies, land-sailor skewed to an Irish passion for magnified

*The Old Firehouse, just across the street from the new, on Paran Creek in North Bennington, Vermont, served as a studio for Paul Terence Feeley, the gifted American painter, until his untimely death in 1965, when it was converted into a storehouse for his canvases and a residence for his wife—and more recently, a sublet for friends.

miniatures, miniature magnitudes—alternate symmetries
of the old wood-worshipers building with megaliths or
lacing the finical borders of the Book of Kells—bending your forms
with the precarious delineation of metal hammered thin and painting
the absences: fastidious illuminator: the shipwreck
on the Firehouse floor is not for you, beached for the night
like a clipper under gauzes and tarpaulins and butcher's papers.
I cannot bear the striking of your colors, that Sargasso of
passionate forms.
            But sometimes from your sun deck I have seen
a crazy armada, canvas over canvas, break a storm
of sails, climb the stair to the millrace and the esplanade
of barns, burn with Egyptian extravagance in the maples
and window-glass, tacking toward Cydnus to call you from the dead
and paint our northern autumn with Pompeian red.

2. *Cat's Cradle*

Something the cat watches from his
cradle, in Ishmael's image,
his ear laid lightly
in swatches of cross-hairs, like a
marksman sighting
a target of silence, the circuits
of a stethoscope's medallion,
looks back at the cat in midsummer
lightning and waits at a hole in the dark.

Something cavernous, cloacal, rank,
like a breathing of grills in a sewer
or a failed
stem in a glass
that thickened into mucus and then
stank; the frog on the well's floor, winy
with compost, ringed with ovulation;
the sac in the prawn's side, gorged;
the leaven in the whale's lump and the slime.

Dilating or sheathing its claws,
whiskered and spiked
like a Hapsburg, paws to his
ruff, with his eye-hairs
hiked in a vector, paring time
with his eye-slits,
the cat, from his crow's nest
on the creek bank,
predatory, tactical, binocular,

genius of speculation, feels
for a cause in the dark—
slippage of glaciers
and Precambrian corings, a
sleepwalking pigeon
shifting his stance or his feathers,
the mouse's tooth in a platen
of marrow, jeweled
on a hairspring of leather: feels

with the whole of his instinct,
dinosaur and serpent diminishing
to a purr—the whole
encompassment of darkness, invisible
ripenings like the bloom
on the underside of a leaf, darkness's
mother wit rising and falling, the bough's subtle
breathing where noon is thickest—whether to
magnify being or make our nullity rich:

the cat will tell you which.

for Jack Moore

3. *A Suicide: Paran Creek*

Cleopatra: Give me my Robe, put on my Crowne, I have
Immortall longings in me.

i.

The granny glasses under
the blind earpieces
folded over, the untimely cobalt
coat, quartered
into itself, and the painful
cane in the starved
March grass—put by
in decorous self-murder—

everything seemed urgent—

even the scum on the creek bank
where the millrace
smoked under flotsam
smelling of horse-piss, sour lumber,
detergent—

as, punctual to a fault,
you stayed to look your last
at the ordered streetlight, cropped
like a crozier, the Firehouse clock
in the car-barn
with its cunning pageantry of hoses,
its ambulance in yogurt and enamel
that might suddenly shriek,
whirl in a carousel—bells or
blood roses—

and with no hope
of manageable disaster—

you leaned to a muddy bottom,
all your length, face

down, as you would read
a hieroglyph of cancer and arthritis
and acedia, and left a floating answer
in the morning.

ii.

(Yet something warmed you strangely
for a moment—a midsummer trick of swallows
over water, the trout's
whiplash under a shaking rainbow,
a black cat on the newspapers
and comics where a child
bought licorice strings—

or the "immortall longings"
of a sister who wore
Seleucid's stolen
bangles under her pharaoh's robe,
flinched in contrary cold: *"Your*
crown's awry; I'll mend it
and then play. . . . ")

while you, her diffident neighbor,
alike in longing,
faced the other way at one
or two in the morning, hard-
hearted, anachronistic,
put off your steaming glasses
in Alexandrian blood-heat,
the blue, unseasonable coat, and
the cane beside them—just
as your note foretold—
and were delivered down.

4. *The Double-Goer: North Bennington*

i.

Seeing that dangerous mover,
we remembered the hazards of walking again:

the mastodon's trick
of stacking his spine on its child's box of blocks;
the mantis's walking stick;
or the equilibrist
bearing down with the webs and the soles of his feet,
claw over crystal, and printing a town with his fists,
isometric, saurian, prehensile,
moving toward plunder.

ii.

Face to face
with that obdurate profile pointed one way only,
drawn to its length like a bowstring,
with the noose
of a tie underneath, and a hatband
to level his jaw to the set of his teeth,
an arrowhead flinty with mourning,
insomniac, lonely—
coming or going we averted our glance when we met
and offered our backs to our guilt.

God help our uneasy walkers, we said. God hold
their weight to the invisible wheel
of their feet driving their anguish uphill
in all weathers; tether
their toes to the chains
moving over and under, tighten
the tendons and ratchets.
God true their purchase,
walking past taverns and graveyards in a hemorrhage
of leaves or the herringbone blue
of the snow. God make their placelessness perfect, going
nowhere, wherever they go.

iii.

Where should a man walk in his fear and his need?
The gymnopede
walks out of his innocence into his vertigo,
rises and falls on his toes,

knowing all distance is mortal, all walking
demonic. The wanderer, trying his exile over and over,
measures his failing humanity,
and the stalker intending him harm
circles the sufferer, crumbles a spoor with his fingers,
and walks toward the print of his prey.

Only the walker keeps earthen.

The saltimbanque,
tumbling toward God, falls another way. The swimmer
working in fathoms, the breaker of ether,
alter their stance to their element
and forsake the old Adam. What was vertical,
durative, perishing,
falls like a diver or floats on a stilled horizontal.

Only the walker totters past the rattles and mats
of his childhood, erect, toward the sexual flaw
of his symmetry, goes frontal,
and doubles his burden.

iv.

Even pity is helpless. Should we question
the bartering God—supposing
all action were fable, all
being, beginning: a "Prologue in Heaven"
or a charade for two players
bent over their pawns,
the unmoved movers of a dice-cup shaken by good and evil:
should we ask, midway in the walk:

"Why go looking for trouble? Why
lengthen your distance to hate us? Where do you walk?
Where are you from?"
—the answer already is given,
Belial's or Baudelaire's: "*From*
going to and fro in the earth and walking up and down

in it. I am your Adversary,
homicidal or prodigal, Dutchman
or equivocal Jew, practising life. I am Ishmael—
your brother, your double, your Other."

SOLITUDES

*homage to Antonio Machado**

1. *Fat Tuesday*
Yesterday's
seven-thirty still clots the bandstand
clock. A child sleeps near the tinsel and papier-mâché
in a kerosene ring under the wavering flies.
The lovers embrace on the grandstand

as slowly
the machinery of celebration engages
its spokes and wheels around the incandescent center
of their pleasure. The plazas sparkle like stages
with a blind bicarbonation, and the masquers enter.

How simply
their dangerous reversal
is accomplished, the permutations of concealment
turning the cheesecloth and the mica of their disguises
into the dramatis personae of a dress rehearsal

and showing
the eyeholes' razor edges framing the double ovals
of the masquer's eyes, like buckets re-arising in a well, glowing
with vagrant spontaneities, the amateur's surprises
caught in the act of his improvisations.

Knowing
those Tuesdays of the flesh, reptilian
in their hungers, Antonio Machado, dragging his horsehair
greatcoat, his *Irregular Verbs for French Beginners,* the chalky
bastinado of his calling,

*Antonio Machado (1875–1939), Spain's greatest master of the "Generation of '98," lived out a widower's life of deprival as a teacher of French in the secondary schools of Baeza, Soria, and Segovia, and died in exile in France toward the close of the Spanish Civil War. Among his final works is a volume of "apocryphal poems" and a collection of prose—"epigrams, maxims, memoranda, and memoirs" of an "apocryphal professor" in whose guises as Meneses, Mairena, and Martín he disclosed the erotic and philosophical preoccupations of a lifetime.

through the parched
Castilian school day, in earshot of a parish's explosion,
scribbled a maxim in his *Marginalia:*
"Not to put on one's mask, but to put off one's face: that
is Carnival. The face alone in the world—that is appalling!"

And watched
from a cindery tussock how the masquers circled
a fountain in Baeza, putting off his cheekbones, eyes, the sensuous
underlip, emptying his skull of what it held
under the make-believe regalia,

leaving only
the armband of the widower's long deprival,
the schoolteacher who had "studied under Bédier and Bergson"
counting martlets between the bell tower and horizon,
intent on the apocryphal and lonely.

And noted:
"The poet is a fisher in time: not of fish
in the sea, but the whole living catch; let us be clear about that!"
He put off his face, facing away from Madrid. The Tuesday of the guns
grew fat.
He crossed the border into France, put on his mask and died into his wish.

2. *Boiling the Egg*

> *Poetry is the word in its time; and students of poetry must maximize the temporality of their verse. . . . All our class exercises have been devoted to this end. . . . I especially remember a poem called* Boiling the Egg.
>
> —Juan de Mairena

On that morning of his exile
there was a sound of gunshot and zarzuelas from a nondescript
cantina. He looked toward Soria and Segovia, comedian
of the grieving countenance, packed his bag for France, and scoured his
table-top
like an apothecary

to boil an egg. All
was in readiness: the mourners and personae of a lifetime—Meneses
and Mairena and Martín—the pestle and the mortar
of a broken boyhood, his widower's thirst, with its bucket on a ratchet
by the well, and a wheel

to draw his dearth up
from the cypresses and solitude of Castile—and, for his last vagary,
the battered barber's basin of a hero, sand from the caves of Montesinos
to measure off the minutes of his hourglass; and the egg
shaped like a zero.

He lighted his spirit lamp,
candled his whimsical egg, as for some feat of prestidigitation,
turned back his watch-dial's fatal circuit to cancel out
the day, climbed the college ramp to erase a pedant's quibble—"*Dasein*
into *Néant* into *Nada*—"
and began his peroration:

"That we must wait until the egg
boils or the door opens or the cucumber ripens is
something that merits your reflection, gentlemen!" The listeners drew
closer.
"Democritus moves the atoms in the Universal Egg. But the boiling of
the water
is the work of Heraclitus. It is

irreversible." And yet, how easily the boy
from Chipiona might have sucked that egg, blown out its white and yolk
through a pinhole in the shell, filled the void with perfume or confetti,
circled the circling lovers in the six o'clock *paseo,* and smashed
the oval on a darkening carnival!

The egg boiled on, with none to see
the bloodlines in a map of Europe hardening in albumen,
the yolk melt down the crown of Montezuma, the caciques
of Isabella drink the steam up like a mushroom, Hiroshima's tissue-paper
skies catch fire in the conflagration.

He waited till the needle
splintered the spindle in his hourglass and the lingering bubbles ran to
froth.
Only the egg remained, unscathed and disimagined in the burning.
Then he pinched the blueing flame with a forefinger, dinted the egg's
perfection,
and moved forth on his journey.

3. *Journey of Abel Martín*

after Antonio Machado

i.
Circling the bell tower,
the martlets, trailing, soar:
children are storming the air and crying at their wars.
Adept in his solitude, Martín, in a corner there.
Evening or twilight making, dust
and a squabble of voices, a child's vociferations—
fifty or twelve, however you make it, all's one.

O starveling spirit and prodigal of soul,
by the glowering bonfire's circle
where dead sticks crackle in a fiery air
and blazon a blind frontier,
showing its blackest cicatrices clear!

The living shall surely perish, as Abel said.
Ah, distance, distance! the star
that none may handle, yet lightens the way ahead:
shall any voyage prosper, lacking it?

Great eye that looks on distance—O lessening sail!
heart indurate in absence,
bland herbs
and honeys of love, blessed in forgetfulness.
Lore of the mastering Zero, of the rounded

fruit's quintessence ripening for man's need,
gout that breaks in a dream, and fountainhead of shadow,
shadow of godhead under the stretched, dread hand!
Before it be Day, if day be given, indeed,
the all-beholding light that is not yet come to pass,
whelm what is vile in me, outcry and exhortation,
Lord of all essences, and drown me in Nothingness!

ii.
And that angel, skilled
in his secret, went out to Martín in the pass.
He gave him the little he had—the pietist's
pittance, perhaps? or a sop for extortionists?
Perhaps. But Martín there in the cold
knew himself lonely, strove with his knowledge, reproved
the Omnipotent Knower Who had no eye for His child,
and all that night in unspeakable wilderness moved.

iii.
And saw his equivocal Muse
erect by his bedstead, the fugitive
haunting his streets, the bereft
and impossible love and the lady forever beloved.
And called to her: Lady,
for the uncovering of that face, my passion
thought to live until morning,
though my heart's blood turn to suet.
Wisdom is given me now. You are other than I dreamt.
Yet would I bless you still
and gaze the more, however you walked at your will,
at my side, in cold contempt.
                                        Death turned to smile
at Martín, but knew no way to do it.

iv.
I lived, I drowsed, I dreamed—
Martín thought, while his pupils thickened—
and thereby conceived a man in a slumbering vigil

intent on his dream, beyond what is dreamt or imagined.
Yet, if a harder reckoning be wanting,
equal for dreamer and watcher alike, and the same
for those who apportion the roads
and those who follow them, panting,
conception in perfect nullity is yours, in the end:
the shadow of your presence, a colossus,
divinity left gazing at us blinded.

v.

First anguish; then exhaustion,
the pangs of despairing assurance:
the unappeasable thirst no water may ever diminish,
wormwood of time made poisonous with durance.

That lyre stretched for his dying!

Abel made trial with his hand
of his emaciate body.
Beholder of all that exists, did His vision not see him there, lying!
O the sloth of it, bleeding oblivion!

Help me, Lord help me!

His life, from its beginnings,
the unchangeable fable of his being, hovered,
traced on the yielding wax.
Would he melt, with the coming day, in the sun?
Abel lifted a hand
to the light
of the vehement morning reddening into summer
that burned on the balcony of his diminishing habitation.
Blinded, he groped for the glimmer he had never discovered.
Then he raised to his lips,
grown icier now, unhurried, the immaculate glass
of purest dark—O purest darkness!—brimming.

THIS SCRIBE, MY HAND

When this warm scribe, my hand, is in the grave.
—John Keats

1.
You are here
on the underside of the page,
writing in water,

anachronist,
showing your head
with its delicate fuses,

its fatal telemetry,
a moundful of triggers and gunpowder
like a field-mine,

your sixty-one inches
and your gem-cutter's fingers,
anonymous,

taking the weight
of a "roomful of people"
but making no mark,

pressing the page as I write,
while the traffic in Rome,
demotic with engines and klaxons,

circles the Pyramid of Cestius,
crosses a graveyard, and submerges
again like the fin of a shark.

2.
I write, in the posthumous way,
on the flat of a headstone
with a quarrier's ink, like yourself:

an anthologist's date and an asterisk,
a parenthetical mark in the gas
of the pyramid-builders,

an obelisk whirling with Vespas
in a poisonous motorcade.
I make your surgeon's incision for

solitude—one living hand, two
poets strangled in seawater and phlegm,
an incestuous

ego to reach for
the heart in the funeral ashes,
a deathbed with friends.

3.
Something murderous flows
from the page to my hand—
a silence that wars

with the letters, a fist
that closes on paper: a blow
with the straight edge of a razor

that falls with a madman's
monotony; or the adze
of a sleepwalking Sumerian

nicking the wet of the clay,
hacking a wedge in a tablet
in the blood and the mica,

till all glistens with language.
The criminal folds up his claspknife. The shutters
slam down on the streets. *Nobody listens.*

4.
Out of breath with the climb, and
tasting a hashish of blood,
what did he see on the brink

of the Piazza di Spagna? A hand
in the frame of a cithara
where beggars and sunbathers

clotted the levels like musical
signatures, a Wordsworthian
dream of "degree," "unimaginable

time" touched by an axe
blade—or a pram
on the Steps of Odessa

torn from the hands of
its mother, gathering speed for the
plunge and rocking its tires

in the rifling, like a gun barrel,
smashing its way through the Tzar's
executioners, to a scream at the bottom?

5.

A failed solitude . . . The bees
in the Protestant grass
speak of it delicately

in the sweat of a
Palatine summer, guiding my hand
through the Braille of the letters.

Violet, bluet, or squill—
what was it I picked
under the epitaph, what

rose to my touch
in the thirst of the marble, a cup
from the well of your grave

in the noonday miasma,
a hieroglyph in the water, saying:
solitude, solitude, solitude:

you have it at last—your
solitude writing on water,
alone with its failure.

6.

You are there
on the underside of the page,
a blue flower in my Baedeker,

writing on water. I know it.
The paper pulls under my pen
peaks into waves

running strongly into the horizon.
The emptiness hardens
with balustrades, risers, and levels,

a staircase of Roman
azaleas. I slip on the blood and the ink
toward the exigent bed

of a poet. All is precarious. A maniac
waits on the streets. Nobody listens. What
must I do? I am writing on water,

blazing with failures, ascending,
descending among lovers and trippers.
You are pressing me hard

under the paper. At Santa Trinità dei Monti
the stairway parts like an
estuary, rises and falls like a fountain.

There is nothing to see but a death-mask, your
room in an island of risers and treads, oddly
gregarious, an invisible hand in the granite.

7.

The tidal salts drain on a living horizon,
leaving a glare on the blemishing
paper. The silence is mortal.

Nobody answers.

for Joan Hutton Landis

BLOCK ISLAND: AFTER *THE TEMPEST*

Lie here, my art!
—Prospero

1. *Block Island Crossing*

What is't? A spirit?
It carries a brave form. But 'tis spirit.
—Miranda

Crossing at Point Judith, one feels the world's
doubleness in the walloping stance of the Ferry—
Elisha's marvelous flatiron afloat in the fog
like a prophet's token: the boat and its baggage,
its plucky machinery, its cautionary noises,
swampy or soft-spoken, dividing the watery
flannels without wrinkle or seam, to their destination.

Below, inlanders, islanders. A stable
of station-wagons. The cold-drink and the hamburger
concession with its branding-iron's sizzle
of stabbed bicarbonation, mustard in tumblers
under a gable of bulbs.
                                        Outside, the yielding opalescence
and the steam, the nearly visible folding and unfolding
of the spaces, fog in its thermal channels
scudding the levels with a gull's evasions,
flying its semaphore of noises, bell-
clappers, conch-sounds, to a clutter of island pilings.

For suddenly, it is *there!*
                                        Somehow, in the drenched
displacement, a boat no bigger than a haddock
asserts its ungainly will to cross, with its gimcrack
universe intact, endures its self-effacement and its loss
and heaves a hawser to the opposite landing.

                                                        The Island
waits, placed and substantial. What was double or indistinct—
the rose-hip and the cranberry and the pure precipitation

that effaced them—merge in a common passion for existence.
Headlands and beaches, the Lighthouse in the middle
distance, open their burning vectors on the water,
with a map-maker's precision, circle the air
with soundings to say where the rock was ambiguous,
the Ferry's bow and the Village, a single vision.

There is light on the bluffs and light enough in the berry.

We know what the dove knows in our casual
chaos.
                The gangway is down.
                                        A mountain dries for us.

for Mary Jo Shelley

2. *Southeast Lighthouse*

> *. . . teach me how*
> *To name the bigger light, and how the less.*
> —Caliban

Chaos is always there. The Lighthouse's gesture,
poised on its needle, sweeping a compass's foot
three hundred and sixty degrees in chalk and acetylene,
mapping, unmapping, sowing and scything the air,
erasing the seas, tells us in freezing graffiti:
the chaos is there, it is there!

Night shows us a blind man's cane—light tapping the rocks
of an arranged interior whose dangerous threshold is fixed
in a salt parabola, so the keel may not utterly drown
in the doorway, the seven white and eight black blocks
of the headland not suddenly reverse themselves, the watcher
hallucinate and go down

as the furniture of ocean pitches us toward a window
where the slain eye looks at crazy tungsten raking
the zenith with its platinum track, Toledan or Damascene, raw
with the burin's filings—seeing nothing
yet mapping a lane in the brine where Oedipus or Lear
might walk as though they saw:

Saw the ship come unbroken to the pilings, as if
it had learned something of the plummet; saw the skeptical cities succumb
in the night of punishing water; saw chaos itself
at last, unmoved by the word of God, while the face
of the deep still looked out of darkness toward a negative
finger, and was dumb.

For nothing has been created. Nothing! Nothing! All is yet to come.
The cloud that whirls in the Lighthouse's vector confirms
the superstitious dream of Adam and the geography of danger,
the staggering keel in the shipwreck, the gull's wing bloodying glass.
The ocean spins emptily. The Lighthouse counts three hundred and sixty
    degrees. And the salt
comedy of unknowing begins.

3. *Soundings*

> *I'll drown my book!*
> —Prospero

i.

The sea closes like a plum
on its stone. It will presently fall.
Halfway toward Newton's head

it shows a nap of numbers,
rosettes for the navigator,
under the mariner's glass, a gooseflesh of soundings—

a flat map where gulls enter
reading the fine print in tawny aquarelle. Later,
that ripping of edges

at the Lighthouse's base, a pounding
of tumblers and bells in the coarse salt,
the reef in its necklace of skulls.

ii.

Whales work. A swan, leading its cindery cygnets,
sees transparently down
to the center: Alice's tears, the nausea of Rimbaud,

green gall and spittle
to pucker the sea floor, constellate
polyps in the flinty asparagus,

the unsuffocating flora
where the diver's heart explodes
in cross-threads of mica and the sardine throbs like a hummingbird—

all the bright business of darkness
I would read in the charred scrolls, the double pillars
of vellum, crossing with chariots, like Torah.

iii.

The parachutists lie where they have fallen
on mandalas of terry-cloth. The sea has cast
them up like anemones, split prismatic canvas

in spinnakers of beach umbrellas. A sound
of drowned transistors, gulls' claws in the froth,
a lifeguard's whistle, the breathing of pontoons,

hisses through the noon's bicarbonation.
Light hardens the facets. But there, in the sleeper's
eye, the glacial emulsions of a camera,

sight keeps its core of darkness—
an apple halved, and in the satin pockets, point
touching point, like Indian paisley, the seed shaped tears.

iv.

What holds the eye to its salt, Orphean
lookers-back, Sodomites, ruminants
licking a briny meniscus—

what? The pastures of plankton,
coffined nerve-gas, sarcophagi
lifted like thistle three miles under,

are not as inland meadows are. There,
green goes aerial, drives star over star through the chicory,
stays nowhere, asks nothing of the malcontent. But here?

Something unappeasable
in the blond marination of whips, melancholy
bearing night in its bile: an expectation of black.

v.

Failures! The thunderheads of bracken
rise over minefields, the sea burns
like a slum, sends arabesques of oil

on all my summer salvage:
young losses, nightmares, a kneecap smashed,
or a back, forfeiture of sons,

the wild severity of poems,
the mouth's sanctuary, the Mona Lisa smile
of adolescent bellies sloping toward their sex,

drowned fathers, photographs, translations
in the middle kingdom of the languages—
fog, foam, hallucinated form.

vi.

Noah's drunken dream: the animals in twos,
delineated water, rainbows. Fog works in the mummy-cloths;
the sandspit goes, in its spiral nebulae of boulders,

the millrace of the upper air, flying
iodine, the binnacle's
mathematics, battlefields of bathers,

the Pharaonic sun that calcifies the beaches
and cuts the swimmer's diamond in the sand,
the light dividing water from the land,

matter, motion, mind—all goes to bandages,
equinoctial steam. The floating bobbins empty,
bearing the corpse of darkness toward the ocean.

vii.

Block Island, Black Island;* Pablo, Prospero—
how utterly the landmarks tarnish!
Our "residence on earth" shows spiracles,

watery torches, sharks' fins, the purgatorial jaw
of Jonah's disobedience. *It is time*
for the breaking of wands and books.

The rose-hip looses
its petal on the blackberry's dagger
under the certain apparition of a ship,

and I enter the desolating soda
again, taking the whole weight of the sun upon my skin
to drive the darkness in.

for Pablo Neruda

*Isla Negra—Black Island: the Pacific retreat of Pablo Neruda

4. *Freshwater Pond*

Where the bee sucks, there suck I.
—Ariel

The parting of waters should make
a swarthier sound than this:
a noise like the breaking of bronzes
in alluvial silt, Rameses'
chariot wheel, the tambourines
of Deborah and Judith,
Armageddons, hosannas—

but here where the wars of bayberry and peat
sweeten the whole of a promontory,
invisible hexagons meet
in a swarming of salts,
driving their honey and gall
through the core of a continent's
fault, to hum like the wax of a hive.

The line of the spit, where the
snapping turtle and monogamous swan
forage for sugar, glares in a jungle
of cattails. No one can say where
the salt of the juggernaut stalls,
or the bland and the bitter cross over
to mesh like the grids of a sieve.

Yet heavily, heavily one way the facets
of brine drop their plummet's weight
in vaults of acidulous bracken
to harden in iron and manganese;
and the other way the sweets in the rose-hip
climb up a thicket of seeds and leaven their wine
on the summit for Ariel's pleasure.

for Virginia Carlin

5. *A Choppy Sea*

All corners else o' th' earth
Let liberty make use of. Space enough
Have I in such a prison.
—Ferdinand

The world's containment, provisional
as porcelain or crystal—a cup's
clasp on an abyss
or the upward look from a gorge
through a fillet of leaves at Andromeda riding the zenith,
Tiepolo's goddesses skewed on a dome's
umbilicus—persuade us we are finite and bring us at length
to an ocean balancing an island like an egg in a spoon.

Shelf over shelf, the continent offers its brim,
gathers in basins and columns,
a rising and falling of wells,
Corinthian water or the pillars of Angkor Vat. Spending
and replenishing itself, the void fills like a bucket,
the ocean creaks and goes taut,
a dipper empties, and the fountains of Genesis
soak their way through the cisterns and blacken the ledges.

The gull sees it with a predator's
excitement: confinement's opposite angel, overplus,
that lives on the thirst of the starved and abstemious.
Over the platter, the pitcher: the pit of the cataract,
windlass, the trough and the pail,
the underground spilth of a world that feeds on excess
and shows the way to the depths—
the granaries under the shale and the magnets
that sleep in the forms,
pulling continents, islands, messengers, into the eye of the storm.

But nothing will happen today.

A bather stands on a sandbar feeling the sinister
freeze at his ankles. A sailboat tightens its cloths.
High tide: with a tarry light in the greens.
A foaming of potsherds, anthracite flaking the spray,
Indian arrowheads.

Three forty-five. The ferry is punctual.
                                        The pylons yaw
and give way.
              It is a choppy sea.

6. *Nighttown: Block Island*

> *Here's neither bush nor shrub to bear any weather at all, and another storm is brewing.*
>
> —Trinculo

Nothing will happen today. The clammers
are back from the sand-flats, with crystals of chitin
and silt in the slats of their buckets.

The yachts have gutted their catch in the Basin,
slashed filet and roe from the fishbones and construed
all the entrails. The haruspicies are good.

The lights go out at Ballard's and Baroni's. Trinculo
lies down in his litter of six-packs to dream of banquets and noises.
The adolescents pair off in the lutheran curfew.

The streets stream toward an ocean mapped out with
nautical numbers. In the lattices of porches the Lighthouse's helix
hones its façade of Victorian scrimshaw and gingerbread—

all the banked transportation of bicycles,
boathouses, bell-buoys, triangular flags to point
to the weather tomorrow, blind polaroid, sun lotions.

Only the headlands show garnets and blues,
a tunnel of melting graffiti fogged with initials
and gases—submarine, subterranean.

But something is pulling the pylons
askew in the underground cities, gnawing away the foundations.
The plumb lines that fasten the tides to the craters

and calculate deserts are tilting a continent's biases.
The oceans are drying to peat on their shelves, the peat into cinder
and flint. Chaos is showing its hearth-bed of iron

again, black holes and barnacles, the fiery maw
of a starving leviathan. In the dark of the morning
a planet is turning to ether, as midwinter landscapes

efface themselves under snow. An island is going
to blubber and fin, a garbage for krakens, streamers
of pitchblende, coronas. There are warnings.

All hangs in the balance. All waits for the
rubbery boots of a swordfisher, a deckhand to fold the drowned
tarpaulins and open a lane to Portugal.

Ariel comes with his tray for the drunkards
in a thicket of berries and cutlery. Big-bladdered, they stand
to the arch of their urine, caryatids supporting a rainbow; and

nothing will happen today.

III

NOWHERE BUT LIGHT

(1964–1969)

There is nowhere but light.

THE ORANGE TREE

To be
intact and unseen,
like the orange's scent
in the orange tree:

a pod of aroma
on the orange's ogive of green
or a phosphorous voice
in the storm of the forge and the hammer:

to climb up a ladder of leaven
and salt, and work in the lump
of the mass, upward and down
in the volatile oils of a wilderness heaven:

to sleep, like the karat,
in the void of the jeweler's glass,
yet strike with the weight of the diamond—
perhaps that is to live in the spirit.

So the orange tree
waits on its stump as the wood of its armature
multiplies: first, the branch, then the twig in the thicket
of leafage, then the sunburst of white in the leaves, the odor's epiphany.

All burns with a mineral
heat, all hones an invisible edge on the noonday, while the orange's scent
speaks from the tree in the tree to declare what the holocaust meant:
to be minimal,

minimal: to diminish excess, to pare it
as a child pares an orange, moving the knife through the peel
in a spiral's unbroken descent, till only the orange's sweat,
a bead of acidulous essence, divides the rind from the steel:

perhaps that is to live in the spirit.

DOG IN THE MANGER

Thunder has driven us
where darkness interprets the animal—
under the shears and the picture frames,
the gardening gear in the cellar—
to a furnace in banded asbestos
ticking its waterdrop sounds,
mop-cords of hardening naphtha,
pulverized ram's horn dung.

There lives the crazed and unkillable
gift of her vigilance, the creaturely
fear that tightens the line of her jawbone,
while her fangs in their tortoiseshell
markings draw me into her skull
in a shine of bitumen
and we know ourselves frightened. We are stopped.
We look back toward the pillars

of garbage alive in the working aluminum,
storm-windows stacked, copper
and iron and oil, the gout of the gas
honing its tooth with a midsummer
midge's sound, to the troglodyte's world
that lies under the world of the human.
The house that she carries somewhere
on her back—a totem

of excrement, a shipwreck
of clapboards and shutters, an ark
that boils on the froth of the gutters—
rises and falls on its drains
while we watch for some presence
that troubled the waters. The darkness is heavy,
with a smell like a spade's wedge.
Our spittle is dry. . . . We ride over the edges

together, and I call through the darkness:

Here, Daffy!

Here, Daffy!

CHIPMUNKS

The sweet playfellow
is already aware.
Taking a safecracker's stance
and turning the tumblers of air,
his paunch set down
like a reticule,
his ballerina's eyes
sootily bowed back
as for *Swan Lake,*
dancing the word for surprise
with his henna behind
and the tungsten crook
of his tail, his ears
like an adze
in the cinnamon and black
of his face's triangulations:

what draws love to its object,
unlike to like, impure to pure,
as my eyes to this?
The chipmunk, balancing the spike
of the acorn on prayed paws,
knowing the stations of the rodent,
finds kernel and meat
with his nose,
like any other rat,
and packs the pulp home
with his jaws.
By wainscotting and sewer
a killer keeps his vigil
by a trap:

Love is content with that.

LATE DANDELIONS

The dandelions, wrecked on their stems
in a carnage of tentacles, conduits, and hoses,
clock-faces timed for a morning's explosion
that triggers the wire in the crabweed with its dynamite charges,
and detonates roses,

are a judgment. Crowding the clover and fern,
something demoniac—a gross Babylonian brass
hammered in sunburst and pentacle, Medusan or Coptic by turns—
a puffball of plumage on its way to a savage transfigurement,
is struck down in the grass

and time is made human again. O Angel
of process, who arranges the sequences
and interprets the season: how you wrestled
that night with the dandelion's changes, the wormwood
and work of mutation no watcher has followed,

the fiend in the bag of the mushroom, the corolla's
untimely unreason that forces an ore into feathers,
ravaged the tuft in the bubble, blew a planet away,
leaving only a space where seed after seed gathered,
and a scarab aloft on the stem revelation had hallowed.

ON QUAKING BOG

for Jean Brockway

When the walkers-on-water went under,
the bog-walkers came out of the barberry
thickets, booted in gum to their hips,
in a corona of midges, their ears electric
with sound, beating the stale of the swamp
with their whips and flailing the ground
for the itch under the frond, the fern's
demonology, the mosquito's decibel.

Night-sweat clotted their palms. They tasted
their gall. The sumac flickered a swatch
of its leaves in the lichens and venoms,
a dazzle was seen in the fog
as a vegetal world gave way to a uterine,
pitch pulled at their heels and blackened
their knuckles, the bog-laurel's fan
opened its uttermost decimal and showed them the Bog.

Paradisal, beyond purpose or menace, dewed
like the flesh of an apple with the damp
of creation, the disk of the pond glowed
under the dragonfly's bosses, where a faulting
of glaciers had left it—vaults of bog-rosemary,
buckbean and Labrador tea, a dapple
of leavening mosses soaking in ice-water, peat-wicks
feeding their gas to the cranberry braziers.

They entered the bonfire together. The moss
took their weight like a trampoline:
they walked on the sponge and bitumen without
leaving a footprint. In between,
in the vats of mat-roses where the waterline
closed like a skin, the ambiguous
world of imbalance, non-being, the pre-human
and tentative, was one with the ludicrous.

The quaking began—under their bootsoles
at first, like a whale under ambergris,

then cramming their wrists with a drummer's
vibrations, knocking their ribs and their knees
as all sagged and rebounded. They lurched on the wet
as though tracing a profile of breakers
or displacing the cords and the voids of a net,
and staggered back into their childhoods,

till their feet touched the granite again.
The bog tossed them over the threshold
that opened a path in the spruce toward the opposite
edges. The leaves closed behind them. They walked
an unyielding and tangible world like strangers, remembering
only the hovering glare where the pitcher-plant's
hammer closed on the fly—the light shaking and shaking—
as a pulse touched their feet from below, and passed over.

THE BARRIO: SAN ANTÓN

for Felissa Calderón

1. *The Well-Dwellers*

The hawk hangs in its fathoms
over the wild fig tree
where Doña Porfiria sits in her clerestory of leaves
with an apron of shade and a pasta of wool
on her knees.

Turning the wool
on the square and her spindle of nails, she weaves
skin of the sky on the nude and carnivorous
colors from a ravel of threads on her lap.
A parakeet sharpens its quills on the tin of the cage.
The fig shows its flint
and the ripe avocado
packs its green marzipan under a nap of enamel.

The hawk looks the other way.
A thread in the skein
leads to the gravel pits, the tar-paper splints
and the dovecotes of Atzingo's well-dwellers—
the undesperate poor
whose courts are the floor of the mines: a ceramic
of pumice
when the Falls of Saint Antony lowers its twine
in the drought; or floating its coops and geraniums in midsummer
mud that drops from a cut in the stone
and colors the rooftops with blood.

Doña Porfiria sleeps in a bomb-burst of figs
and ripe avocadoes. The ball on her knees
rolls away to the edge of a precipice
where the Barrio, caught
in its deathly siesta, immobile as bone,
glows on the web of the square.

There is red on the spikes
as the hawk strikes.

2. *The Corral*

The watered-satin
cummerbund of the placed young prince
in the corner of the picture, spread-
legged and slight
in an incongruous countershine of edges—

something out of Velásquez—
a light, maybe,
ashen and rose, that tempers a chalice's
outline, the withers and hocks of the horses,
where armies in an afterglow of straw
await a changing protocol of keys:

something equestrian, courtly, obsolete,
historical cruelty, the subservient upward look
from the stirrups
to the imperial rump in the pommels,
troubles this little corral.

A boy paces the three-year-old,
a thong's length from the nostril's flaring transparency
veined like an orchid.
                                        The animal droppings fall
smelling of iodine and seed, the steam
of the horses' dung, medallions of goldleaf and flies:

As Mexico turns
with a papery sound of bougainvillea,
flashing its doorways and distances—Velásquez's
carrousel—
contemptuous and civil,

and the young prince stares from his dream.

3. *Nativity*

Studying perfection, the charcoal-vendor's wife
scours down her barrack.
                                        For the night of the Child
her table offers to all
the poor man's cornucopia: the syrinx
of the sugarcane, slashed; cut-glass
of *Orange Crush;* papayas laid open,
the anthracite of their seeds and the bonfire of crescents
together;
the shewbread, the crèche, and the knife;
the bed in the dark of the catacomb,
the crossbones and skulls of the peat.

Tonight, the dearth of the world
is immaculate. The cave and the stable
breathe on the birth of an animal,
make perfect their poverty, and the fullness of time
is complete.
Cut-paper mantillas, a tissue of festival lace,
fly from the doorway.
                                    The Child in the bread
and the child in the broken piñata
sit down to their feast of desire and denial
while the candlewick lengthens like tinder.
Even the charcoal is beautiful.
                                                The sticks
drive their roots through the resins, pentecostal
and lost, the oils in the fern
open their scrolls, the bins of bitumen
send a column of myrrh in the soot.

And here is the child of the holocaust, bringing
a cut of the sugarcane!

My hunger is great, and I eat.

4. *Salto de San Antón*
(Saint Anthony's Falls)

We are summoned, we know,
by no great thing—a sound's
excitement, the panache of the spray
on the quill of the waterfall—
to witness some self-expense:
a break in the river's bed
that opens the stone and makes it aerial.

We wait on the cavern's anvil,
not knowing yet
whether to complete or contain or demolish
the thing we would contemplate,
feeling addition and loss, the abyss's overplus,
the hammers of gossamer pounding the feathery glosses
while the stones take a thornier polish—

and the thing we would re-create, the withheld
and the given thing,
convulsive, apocalyptical—
the column of force aloft on the basin's edge
and the bow in the column—
fails in a sickle of water, a glow on the flat of a precipice
like light under a threshold
where the insomniac questioner turning the pages of water,
the troglodyte under the Gorge,
feels the bottomless cold of the source,
the burning away of the brim.

5. *Siesta: Mexico / Vermont*
The light that deals us less
and bears the eyelid down like the pan of a scale
to set our vision right—
predilections of ochre and pomegranate,
the cactus's belly-hairs, the jeweler's wedge
that widens the magnolia's claw—

delivers us blindfold to our upper and nether
senses. Searching transparency, we hear
the turning millstones at the center,
the infinitesimal pumice in the flaw,
curving the lenses, matching the incandescence
of the edges,

piercing the precision
of a moment like a bareback rider's
hoop burning with spikes and gases;
while the antipodal man
turns heavily in midair,
locking his flying foot-soles above and below,

enters the horizon's double ring, the tropic
and the polar fires—an icicle in Vermont
rayed like Guadalupe's mantle, the frost
on the machete's edge—head downward and head
upward, king of the playing-cards,
who sleeps in the slalom's angle with the Mexican.

THE TERMITES

This dust that wakens my dying
with the waste of the crossbeam—sawyer
of darkness that shows where corruption's
serration has worked in the wood

and passed through, leaving blight
on the pillow, tea leaves, coffee grounds:
that lives in the knot and the grain
and rifles a roof-tree of light

with the smut of its daily cremations—
will not stay for an answer. Gomorrah
burns like a matchstick, and the termite's mound
prepares its necropolis

in the cedar and teak of a table.
Under a chair's rung
the axe falls, dead-center, the plummet's cone
goes taut. A pylon of ash, like an

obelisk, widens on pumice. Murder
is worked in the wormwood
and cancer. Herculaneum's
twilight falls everywhere

while we wait for a plausible sound:
millstones; the tooth's edge on
the tooth; lava and mud. The palm
rattles its quills and the world

whirls once like a distaff
filling, bedded in linen and blood,
tensed to its slack. Light
smashes on cobble

for the vendors of sherbet and gelatin who keep
watch on a splinter of sackcloth,
settle their sores and their stumps in Vesuvial
ash, wake once, and go back to their sleep.

THE GORGE: CUERNAVACA

Out of this nettle, danger, we pluck this flower, safety

1. *The Gorge*

The jacaranda's color,
clocking the air like a pollen,
and the poinciana,
the palm's quill and the sprocket of flinty bananas,
come to me from a gorge's Gehenna. There
in the kingdom of ordure,
the bamboo's stave,
explosion of grasses where water is only a sound—
blood knocking a stethoscope, crepitations
that speak for the sybil from a navel of rubble—
the waste of a city works under mangroves
and is forced underground.
All that remains of the starved and appetitive
life, acid and gall, moves down
under feces and bandages, newsprint, a tin-can
necropolis, cat-gas
in the verminous cane, toward a darkness's
center where the rat mills its
plenitude.

I follow the gardens
aloft over gardens, the gush
of magenta, a shuttlecock seedling, toward
jacaranda again.
Yes, it is there, and it thrives.
held by the eye to the cusps of those doubled
volcanoes, the male and the maiden, one lying
drugged under snow, one erect
like a mace of magnolias,
while equilibrists toil on the slopes toward a purity,
soiling the sheath for a toe-hold,
out of eye-shot, and the condor imagines perfection.

Note: *Legend assumes that Popcatépetl and Ixtaccihautl, one vertical and the other recumbent, are male and female principles, respectively. Both volcanoes are visible from Cuernavaca.*

2. *View from the Gorge*

Doré knew this overhang.
He cut
his cortège for the damned on those levels
to carom on the magnets and springs in the banging
of gongs and the lights of his pinball *commedia.*
In his black-and-white
world, the ascents and descents of the Gorge,
the roots, like a fistful of entrails, the hachure
of pitchblende and acid that abut
on that ordered logistics for sinners,
lead to a fall or a forge.
The odds
are already well-known: electric displays for the winners,
and the damned circling down toward the hammers.

What holds me today
is the purgatorial moment, seen small on the opposite side,
on the tilt of the slope where the gardeners
move in the marzipan whiteness, squared off
like a waffle. Quicklime
has dazzled the glass of the greenhouses there,
sugared the ovens of Hansel and Gretel
where a work of redemption begins
in the alternate lines of the cuttings—bougainvillea
and palm on the ledges—blazing giddily in buckets and tins.
Some loving solicitude has motioned the mannikins there
to hover like dragonflies and settle like seeds in the air—
to balance all day
on a long foot, for purchase, with the shorter
doubled into their shoulders—penitential, half mantis,
half angel, on a causeway of manna and boulders.

And the moment suffices.

What lies plane at the top
like a sponge-rubber glaze for an architect's table
or a primitive frieze for a ceiling;

what we guess from below in the clot of the mangroves:
the generations of Rahab, the fires and the basalt of Dante, the bones
of the beast of Apocalypse, Quetzalcóatl
and Grendel in the offal and trash of our sins—
these were an earlier fable.

In between go the gardeners, with the grace of the hummingbird's
balance, who bend to the slope
in the quicklime and flowers, planting knowns
and unknowns, because sun shines exceedingly there
and the spirit is willing.

3. *The Loco-Bird*

The loco-bird flies over the Gorge,
tilts on a scrub-palm, at his metaphysical
angle, looks down from his glinting
propellers, and takes in his prize, at a glance.

All my awe
at the slant and equivocal—all
I have stood on its head in behalf of the wonder
that sharpens the bat's wit and tightens his decibels
to portents and sounds from down under,
is undone by his stance.
Whatever Zochipili heard
in the flint and the scoriae, the loco-bird sees
what is there to be seen:
two quicksilver drops on the cusp of a fern, and a turd.

Back in the tulipan, he rattles his beads
and enamels. Moving out of the downdrafts unawed
by obliquity, all's one to him: a
descent in a maelstrom or a herringbone
climb up a Matterhorn—the loco-bird swivels
his rudders, steadies his keel, and skates off,
Chaplinesque,
on a rink, in the steerage, a spa, an alarm clock,

a lady's emporium, a steam bath with the peerage:
he knows how it feels
to look into the billy and badge of the actual
and veer out of range on his wheels
without ruffling his daily sensorium.

He fills the whole tree with his presence.
His tail-feathers take on the expansive designs
that our grandmothers mounted in isinglass: India ink
on a background of spirals and pampas-grass, absurd in the litter
of florid calligraphy. He blackens the leaves
with the crow's iridescence,
while a sound issues forth from the glitter:
not madness, not the anger
of Timon, or Lear on the heath, but the gratified scream of the bird
of the abjectly ridiculous—a sound like a child's smutty fingertip
rubbing the damp of a shaving-glass; or a glasscutter's wheel
over glass; whistles and burps; an acetylene blast;
and the banging of a safe-cracker's tools in an empty museum.

All tumbles into the Gorge,
bounces off into nothing from level to level, is absorbed in the stream.

It says: *The devil walks to and fro in the world, the devil . . .*

But the bird in the tulipan tree has no answers.

4. *Flower Market*

The divers in Eden go down and return
from the well of the cobbles
with a festival target of flowers,
the roulette of the funeral wheel,
tinfoil, terra-cotta and fern,

in a birdsong of names: *El Clavel,*
La Orchidea, Rosalinda. Hands

work in the runnel of water, like fish,
looping wire in the floating corollas, unreeling
their roses like brackets of sponges, frames

for the wreath of the wicker,
dishes and jars where the honey-bee
strikes with a sound of exploding fuses,
and roots in a bandage of lilies.
A perishing

forest of stems, cut gardens
that fly under awnings and carrousels,
blacken in buckets. The clot
of the scathing carnation bores through a tunnel
of pollen, and falters. Midday

is limp on the stones. A reek, as of altars
and napkins, suppuration, the candlewick
flapping on wax, saints
in a strong-box of bones, charred
rocket sticks, gather like marsh-gas.

Under a groundswell of plaster
the gutters slope toward a cut in the Gorge,
bleeding all color. Water-boys
wilt in the stalls. The shutter slams down
for the shopkeeper's lock. And night festers.

5. *"Gayosso" Ambulance Service: Emergency*
(Cuernavaca to Mexico City)

Feet-last,
on Gayosso's tea-caddy for corpses
and convalescents, all seemed an
"emergency." Already
the colors had charred in the tulip-trees,

batons and vibrations
barred on a cereal zodiac, while I rolled
underneath toward the van
in my onion of blankets.

The idea of non-being,
the broths and syringes, cocoons
of miraculous molds and detergents that spoke
of a "turn for the worse," swirled
in the headlights. The gorges turned backwards,
the city sloped under my shoulders in a rocket-burst
starring the Valley of Mexico. All tripped like a lens and a shutter
on the flare of a moment and spoke for the traveler:

"Urgent!"

Urgent?

And what of the fraud of that "safety?"
The clown climbing the clock in the celluloid,
the tortoise-shelled
yokel brilliant with nausea, caught
on the clock-face, on the pin and the pointer, riding
his belt-buckle, knows better. . . .

One walks as one can
on the vertical planes
of the windows like ties on a trestle,
looking fifty flights down to a dumb-show of
Stock Exchange runners; one slips
toward the tooth of the buzz-saw
while the freight-cars bear downward from Toonerville,
sparkling with danger.

So the scene recomposes itself,
undemure in its aftermath, "drawn to scale."

Having rented a cut in the Gorge
in a weather where even the tiles on the facing embankment

are plain, one endures the precarious.

Always

crossing the tulipans, somewhere
Gayosso's "emergency" rides on the scream
of a moment: the lateral life of the "urgent"
centers and stays on an ego, like a carpenter's bubble;
the equilibrist falters,
shocked by his personal hazard.

But another sound

lives in the Gorge—
an equivocal threshing of bamboo and manure and papyrus,
neither pure nor impure: the spirit
that works in the middle
stark under the sun-stone,
in the mash of upper and nether.

And heard as the Gorge Dweller

hears it, the serpent's tail beating the shell,
that unriddles its birth in the wet and the dark

And says: *It is well.*

It is well.

6. *Full Moon: The Gorge*
With the moon at full, its blind side
falls toward the Gorge, two flint-stones kindling
a glare in sidereal trash: tintops, bottles, and glasses
starring the foliage with the constellation of the Pair—
a pubis of blackening mangrove on a pubis of ash,
a mating of filaments, fatal and beautiful there.

All absent things move toward their fullness now:
all shaping artifacts, essences, human similitudes,
briny or bloody deluges, sweatdrops, semen, and air,
all troubled tossings of parturitive foam

or fiery paradigms that work in the perishing
flesh to dazzle the pulses and sparkle like mustard seeds
for the bird in the animal excrement, the ammoniac singer—

toward that zenith warmed by sunlight, the egg in the down
of exorbitant dark: light's underside,
where the pottering flyer fails on Canaveral
and, one after one, the universes disclose themselves
in the gravitational swamps, as noonday burns to its socket
and is night. Night. Night as I would have it,
night that I sought in its festival guises as sun-stone,
planetary rose, salt with its faceted enigmas, fern,
fires of the sexual whale saying: *I am. I made it!* in
catastrophic sperm, love's underside, love's failings, tears—

yes, love's ignominious reversals that my heart's starvation
would have reversed, if it could: night with its names for powers,
dominations, fears: houses, Homeric fictions: Dante astray
in the tiger-taken wood: Hell with its vortical vengeances:
and night, night without respite or guile, the light of common day.

CUTTING THE BITTERSWEET

for Anne Schlabach

The quarrelers in bittersweet,
saviors and butchers, too late for stealth,
are here in the August morning, in the first of the heat,
with their stilted pruning shears and their puritan hate

to root out the trespasser, berry and branch,
in a country vendetta. They have seen
how the strangler advances with trident and net,
forcing its pod in the thicket of lilac—

the gratuitous killer whose
grievance is everywhere, scribbling the margins
with threats, cutting anonymous letters
in the broadening leaf: who stabs through the stake and the splint

to gather a mangled typography
and extort the whole plenty of summer: the crime
that shows only the glint of its appetite, the red of the bittersweet
berry, to say what catastrophe means

and speak for the mindless destroyer. But justice
is manifest. A pruning-fork works
in the cluster. The noose of the bittersweet opens
its spirals and layers, disengaging

the rose and the poplar and surrenders its murderous
sign: a cutting of ovals and staves,
like a musical signature, a bonfire alive on the stones.
And the searchers in bittersweet—those whom the summer

left nothing, the red-handed ones bereft in a winter
of holly: the parasitical borrowers,
time-servers, counterfeiters, the clingers and late-comers,
gather the harvest indoors.

WINTER POND: LAKE PARAN

for Jo Van Fleet

Lest the ripple deceive us
with its midsummer dazzle, a cat's-paw
of lustre on the shimmering weight of the water,
and the Heraclitean swimmer
dissolve into light, scarring the pond
with its passing—arm over arm in the herringbone ringed with a gas—
and no one believe us:

I stand in the March
of my mind in a winter perspective:
suds, scurf, cobble—a sherbet of blackening ice
with a pylon inset on a lunar enormity, and beyond
it, a tractor in characterless orange:

the lake like an adamant
drawing into the flint and the salt
all a planet's mobility—algae and perch,
the gelatinous hives of the frog, night crawlers,
the semen and freeze of a winter—until
all locks, like a cluster of crystal,
lifts up in its basin in its perfect containment,
a monolith crowding the shale,
a troglodyte's hammer
pounding the weathers and pressing on obdurate matter
like the light on the pomegranate's rind,
or the bones on the scales of a carp.

The seasons disclaim us. But a shock lives on in the air—
a pulse like a forge in a cloud
that beats on the latent and makes the ambiguous bearable.
Facet by facet, we assemble a vanished relation—
the swimmer under the ice and the skater on water—
harden the edge of our world till our images name us
and the possible touches the heart and declares what it saw:
an ice-floe that burned in the thaw,
the hailstone's precipitation

that opened a well for the noon of the fish and the flycaster,
set a bow on the ripple, recovered the spinner's vibration,
till all was motion and passion and presence, flashing as never before:

And the swimmer arose in his nakedness and called from the opposite
shore.

COLD

The clock for the great cold stopped dead.
—Léonie Adams

1.
When cold froze the locks
and the alarm gave no sign of awakening,
I sank underneath, in the wheel-master's well of the clock,

and saw trapped there the great beast of Time
that eludes all the hunters,
poised by a second on the claw of a ratchet, alive in its changes,
beckoning:

the freeze at the heart of the world
unfolding the bone of the fiddlehead
icicle, cornucopias of maidenhair, asterisks of lichen and frost.

My breath stood forth on my face, Job's
spectre, sleeper in causes and compasses,
that hardens a block in the river

for the sailor's dead reckoning
—carborundum and mercury—
and writes in the book of the cold with iron pen and lead forever.

2.
Cold moves in the legs of Socrates, soldier,
and music moves in the hemlock
of the flute-playing gymnast at his games in the mind

where death and its mourning apprentices, after the oracle's
horseplay, nude under glistening oils,
touch on the stones of the bath

with a satirist's laughter, and the sex
unsheathes on its stalk for the young man's dalliance
and the old man's tenderness:

discobolus: the intellectual cold
of the agora in a boy's Spencerian hand
writing circles and ciphers, push-pulls, staves of the musical line

in its freezing calligraphy, thought
working on thought
in a quicksilver column, while the ontological hero

toils on outrageous errands, the stables
are swept at last, and at the apple's end Hesperides
smokes in the rapist's hand: a zero on a zero on a zero.

3.

In the house of the Snow Queen, I remember,
all smelled of acetylene. The strayed child
under the Turkish cupolas

drove the splintering flints of his gaze
over sand-castles and tundra,
his knuckles gouging his eye

snowblind with loss and unable to cry:
while, for the sake of his grief,
cold turned to smoke on the nursery

window, unfolded enormous devices
of deprival and loss, the tree
neither evil nor good, and the cross in the garden of ices,

isometric, pubescent, joining the nipple and navel,
a rainbow boring the salt in a double relief—
an angle of onyx on a circus-rider's spangle,

ascending: a diamond on a diamond on a diamond.

4.

Della Robbia's ceramic: this blue-and-white
hearth-bed of glazes holds no "loves" or madonnas,
plaques of ascending crevasses, reliefs to allure and invite

in a childhood's geography hardened to flour-paste
and traced with a map-maker's line. Nothing amazes.
The fiction of human direction

prints its necessitous footstep in the glare and the brine
and fails in a blind circumspection:
Under the flake and the sparkle

a presence that grapples a continent, the glacier
that walks the moraine, the whole
heft of mica and gravel, alluvial conch and detritus

tilts halfway toward Asia, turns on its axle of coal,
dragging its fish-bones and flint-heads, iron and bronze in the ferns,
slips toward the pole

on a pendulum's backswing. A heartbeat is heard in the rock.
And the cold, the great cold, the geysers of oracular cold
issue forth to the Pythoness.

And a ratchet resumes in the clock.

PAPERMILL GRAVEYARD

(North Bennington, Vermont)

In that country of thresholds we move like vandals,
overturning birth dates, death dates, necrologies, Bartlett's
Familiar Quotations, the exorbitant rhetoric
of compliment, spelling hard names, looking for pictures
under the blackboards of a child's stone library
of aphorisms. In the runt gardens and the greenhouse
"arrangements"—pinwheels of laurel in plastic, jelly-jars
crammed with wildflowers not meant to outlast
an homage, the rancid memoranda of the very poor—
all is remembered. Each gives to each in a ghastly
plenty: the intimacy of a terminal cough
recalled in formaldehyde and licorice, a bull's-eye of death trance,
the husband's abandoned spasm in a barrow of granite,
endearments, betrayals. The tribal successions of the unexceptional man
are plausible here. Even the destitute scribble their heraldries.
The soldier schooled in a captive security, mistrusting the living,
salutes the interrogator with name, rank, and serial number.
Under the chintzy flags, holidays, holocausts, individual
deaths, the unlucky recruit, blinded by chevrons, is caught
in the scintillation of family keepsakes, a rabbit's foot
crossing the spaces in search of savory greens. All
remains minimal: footlockers of Government Issue
cut frugally to size, berry-boxes for the stillborn,
mortuary cabinets indexed under Urgent Business
in an Erechtheum of furnished pillars
where death begets death and nothing comes of nothing.

Having nothing to memorize but an expatriate spirit,
her chemist-husband, married, unmarried, remarried, the epithalamial
rasp of a cello-string and the kindness of friends who covered her loss
with a willow, I forage for trifles—the maggot's hammer-blow,
a lawnmower's blade in the chicory, my face on the bevel
of granite glazed over *"Mother"* and *"Father."*

But this is no trifle.

Jeanne Butler, Jeanne Butler, Jeanne Butler—how strangely you lean
toward the heel of my hand, still living on your nerves, severe in your
Breton

cheekbones, repeating the uvular "r" for schoolgirls from Cambridge,
    settling
your napery while our teacups bitter in a garden
over pitted persimmons broken and eaten together, and a changing wind
works in the wafer's paste, hardens the knife's edge, and delivers
our unhaunted world to the Prince of Darkness!

VETERAN'S HOSPITAL
(White River Junction, Vermont)

Bringing "only what is needed—essential
toilet articles" in a paper bag,
dressed as for dying, one sees the dying plainly.
These are the homecomings of Agamemnon,
the odysseys to the underside of the web
that weaves and unweaves while the suitors gorge upon plenty
and the languishing sons at home unwish their warring
fathers with strong electric fingers.

The fathers are failing.

In the Hospital Exchange, one sees the dying plainly:
color televisions, beach towels, automatic razors—
the hardware of the affluent society marked
down to cost, to match the negative afflatus
of the ailing, the bandages and badges of their status.
Under the sandbags, rubber hoses, pipettes, bed-clamps,
tax-exempt, amenable as rabbits,
the unenlisted men are bleeding through their noses
in a perimeter of ramps and apparatus.

In that prosthetic world, the Solarium
lights up a junk-pile of used parts: the hip that caught
a ricochet of shrapnel; tattoos in curing meats;
scars like fizzled fuses; canceled postage stamps;
automated claws in candy; the Laser's edge; and barium.
The nurses pass like mowers, dressing and
undressing in the razor-sharp incisions
and the flowering phosphorescence. The smell
of rubbing alcohol rises on desertions and deprivals
and divorces. It is incorruptible. A wheelchair aims
its hospital pajamas like a gun-emplacement.

The amputee is swinging in his aviary.
His fingers walk the bird-bars.

There is singing
from the ward room—a buzzing of transistors

like blueflies in a urinal. War over war,
the expendables of Metz and Château-Thierry,
the guerillas of Bien Hoa and Korea,
the draftees, the Reserves, the re-enlisters,
open a common wavelength.
                                        The catatonic
sons are revving up their combos in the era
of the angry adolescent. Their cry is electronic.
Their thumbs are armed with picks. The acid-rock guitarist
in metal studs and chevrons, bombed with magnesium,
mourns like a country yokel, and the innocents
are slaughtered.

                        On the terrace, there are juices
and bananas. The convalescent listens to his
heartbeat. The chaplain and his non-combative daughter
smile by the clubbed plants on the portico.

"They shall overcome."

1966: STONEMASON'S FUNERAL

Shaftsbury Stone Mason and Son Die Under Wheels of Vt. Railway Train While Hunting

—*Bennington Banner* (Vt.), November 23, 1966

1.

"Are you there, son?"

"Here. All here."

I think of the wheels: what the wheels meant:

the cement-mixer by the walled garden,
its conical jet's nose
kneading quicklime, semen, cement,
tilted and turning . . .

and the half-naked ones
seen from above—the son, the father, the son—
filling troughs of cement
at the great wall's center, in the stonemason's way:
the stone rose, the stone heart of the artichoke,
the marrow and block of the burning—

or drinking cold cokes in the cavernous lilac,
the sun on their nipples, their nostrils, their sex,

on their backs, and at rest.

2.

I think of the hunt: what the father was hunting—

paring boulders to bone,
angling and shunting the wedges
of granite, fitting facets like pineapple-rinds, forcing rubble
and shell like flint for an arrowhead—

what was he hunting there, with the hod on his shoulders
and the brick and the straw of the Hebrews behind him,
the Great Wall of China, the tower, the well,

the winnowing wheels and the millstones of Gaza,
the tables of bran and macadam—

What would strike through the granite to find him?

3.
I think of the wall: what the stones meant:

the son, the father, the son,
piling their burial barrow in the nightshade and lilac,
in the cold sweat of Adam:

What blackened the boulders with the horn
of the Scyldings,
circled the rooftops
of Stonehenge, the quarries of Syracuse,
the megaliths
pointing their profiles toward Easter Island
like the dial of a petrified garden:

what were they building
to make an unbreakable world in the dews of the terrace?

4.
"Are you there, son?"

"Here. All here!"

"Keep
your flashes down low. Feel for the brush with your toes.
Drop onto your heels and set them down light.
No use to startle the deer in the dark!"

"Right."

"Watch for the horns of the buck. Stand clear
of the does. We'll double on back
where the path takes the turn by the overhang
and crosses the railroad track."

"Good luck!"

5.
I think of the wheels: what the wheels meant:

the barred box-cars, the freights passing over
a seamed span of track like a carpenter's
rule opened flat to its length
in the gravel and thistle—

cow-catcher, lanterns, and cistern, the rust of the trestle,
the switch—

then a spindle of light like a burning
glass focused on nothing, frosting the clover like glass,
the acidulous smell of the sand on the spikes and the steel
of the crossties—the whistle . . .

till the ruby that held the caboose to its track
spiraled into the jewel of a railroader's watch
and clicked shut—

and the journey was over.

6.
I think of their deaths: what their deaths meant:

having set the last boulder
with the stonemason's cunning that steadies the block
from within, in the pith
of cement, showing only the coarse outer edges, and the spaces
dividing the stones, held in precarious balance
like a zodiac circling the sun—
the son, the father, the son,
pursuing the deer
over crossties of mica like stepping-stones cut for the path
of the steam's effervescence, the whistle, the wheel, and the scream—

having come to the place they had sought: the underground
door in the green of the terraces,
the mastodon's mound in the nightshade and bittersweet:
having said:

"We have seen antler and horn in the labyrinth."

They sealed the great threshold, set the altar-stone over the plinth,
signed the mortar and bricks
with a wreath of initials and three copper pennies

dated: *one nine six six.*

MOON WALK

It is time to re-invent life,
we say, smelling ammonia from Mars
in a photograph, seeing right angles
in galactic soda, a glass bead from a crater,
the color purple.

To that enormous death's head
we bring the constellation of Snoopy and Charlie Brown
in a comic-strip balloon of antiphonal beeps,
with a virus's chemical courage, trailing a ration
of air in Plexiglas and nylon, printing
a square of carbon like a tennis court,
planting our human shadow and contamination.

A hammer taps: *It is later than you think!*

We follow
the White Rabbit through the lunar asparagus,
gathering specimens for the radiologist, peer
into the pockets of Alice's pinafore, grown infinitesimal,
fall into the daydream of the hookah and the caterpillar
and the Sea of Tears.

Still something haunts us from that other life—
di Chirico's light, Dali's pebble seen at six o'clock,
our radical loneliness, our bereavement, our
conspiritorial nostalgia for transcendence. We hear
volcanic tumblers turning in the rock, walk
toward the blinded mirror's other side, and:

"Do not die!"

we say. "Old fire-eater, huntress, menstrual mother,
do not die!

See—we bring you a feather
from that other life, an answering mirror to take
the living exhalation of your breath!"

And wait

by the deathbed for an acknowledging eye
to open, as Wordsworth's children did:

A "simple
Child that feels its life in every limb,"
(the poet said):

"What should it know of death?"

THE ORPHANING

1. *A Failed Rage*

Clear Idiot, I understand.

                                        The adversary
need not be struck, or the blow
returned. Your foreknowledge of the deed
is enough, and proves mighty. You named it Innocency:
the receptive faculty, the negative power, and wore it
under the recoil of the loved hand and the hated hand
falling equally, falling always. You said:
"Yes, I know. The blow comes as I knew it would come.
I foresaw it all. I am not angry." You turned
into your secrecy, smiled for a world's
perfidy, and denied yourself the act.

                                                        All this was false.

The act alone is innocent, and sweetens.
The child strikes with his fist in the womb's haven
and the father replies with the lover's spasm. Spend.
Reply. What was kept has betrayed you. See:
the rage fails, the restorative rage, and the hate
talks with its cause over the infamous pit,
touching nothing.
                                Your awkwardness with tools, all
the gear of action, your poor record at the shooting range,
are the fruit of a denial. Raise the gun to your shoulder.
It is heavier than you knew. Slam the bolt to.
It will not lock to your blow.

Only what is given, is. Only the act returns.

                                                                Be returned.

2. *Ash Mound*

It is time you named your enemy.

Your instruments have devoured you: the poem,
the kiss, the loss, the image, the afterthought,

the orphan in the disinfected playground
crying: *Integrity!* like Job on the ash mound.
Your compass moved upon Self, always, as on a dial,
when you thought to pass beyond it,
magnetic to your incompletion. "Choice"
was a compass's fiction, and "Control,"
only the needle's need to point to the Self
when Possibility opened beyond,
and tremble to a standstill there. Always
volition lay outside, deep in the play of the act
itself—free, bold, availing, neither enemy
nor friend, partial or entire, chosen or compelled.

3. *A Gift of Light*

Mother, in that darkness into which you go,
which is not Lear's or Homer's—not Charon's
bowsprit bearing the devious Florentine
on the downward eddy to allegorical heaven:
nothing dreamt or dissembled, or given the spirit to know,
to prove it precarious, like thirst or the gift of tears,
but blindness itself, a smashing of lenses and lives—
why does my childhood tremble, and my gaze go up
with a child's assurance, for the large, loved hand
of that providing walker who measures her stride to my own
and steadies the balances?

For I guess at a thing
not desolation's, and walk, as toward birthdays, with
all my surprise made ready.

You come with the gift of light,
mulish and brave, in the shine of sabbatical
candles, wearing my blindness: not
in the barbiturate sleep of the maimed, but held in the salt
of a photograph, parting conventional hedges, a rich braid caught
on the serious smile and the Ukrainian stance,
by an apron of porches.

And all is returned in a dazzle, half
seen, like the eyelash's arc on the eye when the sleeper wakens.
Poppyseed burns on my lips. We mount up the kiosk
together, my trust in your hand like a forfeit,
climbing the steps of my nausea
while the bell-tower tips toward the dial of the Orphanage
clock, and the iron opens outward.

There all my sullen deprival
surrenders its lonely disguises.
There is my father,
clear in the long halation; there, the ascending staves of the bed,
harplike, in peeling enamel, where I listen to prodigies:

there,
grave-plot, headstone, prayer shawl,
where the Son of the Blessing arises,
the sevenfold tape on his forearm, and remembers the prayer for the dead.
A stone in the grave of my mouth moves
and I cry from the grave-clout:
Father!

and forgive him his dying, who knew not what he did.

4. *Wedding Dance*
In the Home for the Blind
the ramps plunge under their double harness of rails
like a gymnast's parallels

or a ballerina's barre, to call the blind outdoors
and tilt them toward the gardens. There,
in the tinny brilliance and the braille

of grassy quadrants, my mother waits by the burnished iron
like a dancer by her glass, for the ticking cane,
the cuff-links and the cloth of her blinded dancing partner

that draws her failing balance
toward his arm, opens a lane in soiled, suburban air,
and guides her broken footing through the dance.

The space is full of rings,
thresholds, spikes of flying nylon, dangerous metal,
falls on the netted causeways underneath the swings,

as my mother tries her toehold on the wire,
prehensile as a seabird, breaks out a blind
umbrella, and rides the blazing slant into her *shtetl.*

She has her heart's desire
again—the moon and the fiddle, the night skies
of Chagall, whirled on the thermal currents toward the rafters

in a bridegroom's *pas de deux,*
past Dante's second circle and Abraham's laughter:
"Shall Sara, that is ninety years old, bear?"

My mother holds the tightwire
like a plummet. Her partner, at his ease,
levels the pure progressions of his arc

and tops the trees! His cuff-links glint in the sun. All
is impeccable: the star-turn of the happy aerialist,
flier and flier caught on a stilled trapeze,

till the air is suddenly darker, a wind blows
cold from the used graveyard where, out of my father's eyes,
I watch the dancers print the burnt grass and move into the shadows.

5. *A Stone Raised*

When you turned from us, in your coma,
and we fought on the terrible starch of your bed
to contain your wracked pulse-beat in our circle
of unspoken bereavement,

I heard a sound like the breaking of ash in a crater
where once, in the watersheds
binding my breath to your breast,
knees to my chin,
I slept under your heart—
                                        and I broke from the circle
and said:

> "Put me out of your mind. Put on your death.
> Rest. Grief cannot matter
> in the long degradation
> of blindness, maimed memory lost
> to itself, the great
> faultings of love by which the living interpret
> trespass and probity—all that forces your spirit
> to sweat in the flint and the trash of the earth like a slave
> to win us survival. Take
> up your bed and your grave
> and walk forth to your peace."

Now I would reckon
the whole cost of our greed,
who would have the dead with us—
alive to us only in the indecent duress of their breathing—
because they still work in our pulses.

How much better that the lost and unseeing
should see through our need, in the end, foretell
our heart's changes, pass on to non-being
knowing all would be well with us!

All is well with me, Mother.

Holding the great shell of your heart
in my hands, I hear the whole power of its passion
move through my fears, with its buoys and its bells
in a tilting horizon of undertow:

your blood and your milk still encompass me.
You walk through the gums and the leaves of midsummer,
first at the gates of my Sunday, with a paper
cornucopia under each hand:

There is nothing to own or disown,
nothing left to commemorate,
as now, in the year of your wish,
filling the sky like a birthmark or a ripened placenta,
knowing the rite to be good,
I bend toward your death with this stone.

IV

THE ENEMY JOY

(1955–1963)

How we squandered that ruin of fathers,
And how the inexhaustible fathers restore us!
—"Karamazov"

THE HORNET'S HOUSE

We are the bees of the invisible.
—R. M. Rilke

Upside down on their millstone, the hornets had already begun
That labor for slaves, oblique
Under balancing weights, where their universe hung by a wick,
Till the will of their species was done.

No longer honing their spurs under thorny abdomens
And fording the midsummer, they canted their wings on a slum
Of old parchment, a wafer of smashed candelabrum,
Unweaving and weaving their omens.

Leant to invisible headbands, hods
Of invisible chalk and saliva, some instinct alert to their needs,
Had narrowed their compass to this: assembled them out of the gasses, like
  seeds
On a sunflower pod.

I thought of those others: the bee in his ziggurat, ascending
In savory waxes; the wasp turning his pouch like a fig,
Forcing the rind of his world, like the white and the shell of an egg,
In a pendant's papyrus.

But these, knowing nothing of honey, the Chaldean increases
Of stars in the hexagon, the bells of beneficent amber—
What bounty could kindle their flint in the spoors and the cinder
Of the underground places?

Yet the horn and the needle palpated, made trial
Of their hungers, till a harvest was drawn through their bellies
And rode like the thread in an hourglass, a stinger of waxes and jellies,
And struck in consummate denial

Till everything blazed like a thought, like a sexual breathing of gauzes,
While a kingdom of predators, circling, put forth its antennae
And the poem arose like a hornet, in rabbinical blacks and siennas,
On craters and crosses.

SECOND ADAM

Whatsoever Adam called every living creature, that was the name thereof.
—Genesis

When the Deluge had passed,
into my head, by twos, came the creeping things,
the horn of their jawbones shining, and the things of the air,
wing-cases breaking like clasp knives, asking their names.

Storm-light colored their passing
with an animal imminence. They wheeled
on the pile of their plumage, in the dread of their animal being,
and rode in the ark of my head

where the possible worked like a sea.
Nothing was given me there. Nothing was known. Feather and scale,
concussions of muscle and fur, the whale and the name for the whale
rose on the void like a waterspout, being, and ceasing to be:

till keel clashed and I spoke: *mayfly,*
wood-weasel, stingray, cormorant, mole—
choosing the syllables, holding a leaf to the torrent,
unharmed and infallible, while Creation descended, in twos.

A SALAMANDER SEEN

Salamander
that speaks of our wonder in caustic Sumerian;
whose movement
tilting the summer a moment,
opens a scar in the mica
and stings like the blade of an adze—

serpent that lives in my doubt
on the animal edge of that leap
where the poised and the possible,
nude as a pulse in the sun,
enters the holocaust's ray, breathes upon stone
and sleeps where the darknesses are—

whose depths are the desert
and the whole of that innocence
that smiles at opacity and breaks from the mineral
spray, a dolphin of quicklime and air—

nearer to me than my heartbeat, subtle as frost—

angel of impulse
that leans on its saurian fingers,
abstract beyond pathos; that
eludes the intent of my joy

and is lost.

THE CREMATION: NEW MEXICO

for Eda Lou Walton

I burn a slight body,
placelessly left in my mind, as best I can:
the flower on a cactus's thistle should do it,
or the wilderness fan
where cloudbursts ride on a Conestoga wheel
in summer electric, storm over storm, in a bitter braking of iron.

But a marvel is worked in the sun. The light
that a boy might point with a burning-glass,
singeing the distance with a deckle of papery rust
or curling the print where the smoke of the stylus passes—
carbon and gossamer—poised upon your dying,
masses like Indian turquoise for your ghost.

Your country
breathes in a lion's slumber:
O rise on that furnace of claws
in the bestiaries of your Armageddon,
enter your desolation and your angers,
and walk to Abraham's bosom, through the paws.

THREE COUNTRY SONGS

1. *Wasp and Window-Screen*

An eye on the grained wire
opens the way
from the fern in the drinking-glass
to the shako of lilac.
                                                            It waits
in a lace-maker's frame—a swarmer descending—
moving its needle,
and feeding a bitten margin with the dragonfly's changes.

It would enter a hazardless world.

                                                                                                It would order
the unending, repeated rosette on the lace-maker's border,
and inhabit the center.
                                                                It points its embroiderer's
burin in the nap of the honeycomb, arranges
its wish, and strikes through the web of the sash:

"a peaceable kingdom":
                                                lilac;
a fern in a jelly-jar;
                                                a unicorn
crossing the loom of the window-frame, blood on its horn.

2. *A Stand of Pine*

The hemlock stick keeps its christmas
of midsummers
fox-brush and fishtails of fir,
the demoniac bead of the juniper
building the weathers of Norway, like the cone on its hackle,
in formal explosions, matted starling feathers,

whose green is not strange to us.
We have wrecked
with this whale and his bill-hook before. The bough
sets a luminous spinnaker
on the sleepy bitumens
and tacks through the glosses and gums, like a prow.

Beneath—all a summer's disaster:
the conifer breathing through gill-slits,
a pinwheel of starfish. The hemlock's
spars sway upward, where
deep in the resin and sea-tackle,
the wrack of leviathan stirs.

3. *Tying Tomatoes*

for Rebecca Stickney

Having seen on the staves
that weedy ascension of petals, aerial nightshade,
the green orb under the star
in a bracken of leafage where color awakens,
I climb the tomato, packing the stalks on the stakes,
toward castles and psalters, the magical poultry, and Jack:

And descend, in a game of the casual—
a child's sleepy surprises, a child's commonplaces—
to the other side of the vegetable, the lair
of the carnivore, the killer
of giants,
where the mace of the ogre arises.

The shadow that falls on my fingers,
the sensual frenzy
that thickens the leafage and blackens my thumb-print,
remains. *"Green thumb!"* I say, while the chalk of my knucklebone
numbs under tapwater and the snore in the drain
is chartreuse. *An axe-blade slams in the stalk.*

ANDALUZ

1. *Court of the Lions: Alhambra*
(Granada)

For the monster's simplicity, the menacer's
Way to the center—what but a labyrinth?

The hieratic lions of Alhambra
Circle the court like a map-maker's rose,
In a poodle-dog's tonsure, ferocious, solicitous,
Their muzzles, bared for the water-spout,
Four times scored with a grimace,
Their manes on their powerless shoulders, like a fleece,
Taking the basin's weight on their trumpery toes
Among cameras, talismans, Baedekers, legendary gesso.

Only the lions keep simple.

In the labyrinth's center,
They honor a myth of the instinct's simplicity
With a monster's indifference.
Their savage vocation,
Among pentagrams, figured cartouches, ceremonial plaster:
To humble the conjuror and mock the enchanter
With the unreflective revelation of the obvious.
The minotaur's rhetoric
And all the apparatus of the maze
Fails on their barbarous haunches
And melts in the runneling marble.
Whatever
Has blazoned the arches with calligrams, pomegranates, eight-pointed
stars,
Feathered the mortar
With the peacock's extravagance, surrenders its sorcery
Here in the lion's enclosure.
Here, the invisible ringmaster
That levels the hoop of the fountain's periphery
And lashes a length of cautionary water,
Would have them pigeon-breasted, plaintive, and apparent.

Yet they speak for a fable's conclusion. They prepare
For the bestial deliverer:

"The wands of the Eastern geometer
Are splintered like straw," say the lions. "The cult of the djinn and the
scarab,
The construers of entrails, wishing-bone addicts, compounders
Of formulas, philtres, phylacteries, plain and quadratic equations,
Bow to the lions.

Here, on the portico table,
The kingdom of nuance, the fiends of inhuman refinement
Bend to the fallible animal. Here
The Christian intercessors of our passion,
Armed with an outcry, immediate as a stutter,
Attended by lions, strike through the net and the trident
And batter the skulls of the Arab. . . . "

So say the lions:
While, on their amenable quarters,
The water falls delicate, the enchanter's enigma arises,
Plane over plane and diamond into diamond,
Bossing the surfaces, starring the grain of the panels
With the poet's *Kasidah,**

multiplying columns.

For the place of the beast is bewitched, say the lions.

The channels
Are stained with the blood of a prince's vendetta.
The fountain's thread descends to Evangelist's navel
And charms like a hypnotist's prism.

See: even the marble devises
A sleep for the lions. Whatever their vigil,
Poem and magic are joined in a dream for a savage's pleasure.
Alhambra assembles
Its ascending wasp-nest's heaven
Pouched in the plummeting chalks twenty ways planed

*Kasidah: Arabic verse forms incorporated among the geometric and floral motifs by the Alhambra architects.

To the ceiling's improbable vertex, like a leaven;
Its columns in harvest-clusters, ringed
On the marble's shewbread; in a Musselman's script,
Cursive and flourishing, repeating a violent fable
In the semblance of bowsprits, wheat-staves, cutlasses,
Hummingbird vibrations.

2. *Alhambra Gardens: Kasidah*

Blindness at brightness's center. The enchantment
Would have us blind. Else why,
In the Hall of the Sisters, where the loom of the wall grows intenser
And vision turns, rapt, for its answer,
Does vision surrender its witness, the eyelid repel
What the artist had shaped for the eye?
Why does our vigilance fail
And deliver the magic for touch to interpret, like Braille?

Deprived, at abundance's center, surely
The lords of complexity guessed at the simple?
Else why, in the maze of the caliph's arcana,
Where flower and fountain are wed to a temple's example,
Did the gardeners labor so purely
To flatten the cypress and level the plane of the fountain
For the noon of a concubine's slumber
Or the arm of a floating sultana?

3. *A Grape Tasted: Málaga*

The seed
seen black in the green
bloom, like a wick under frost, the oval
flawed where the grosgrain
parts for the twig in a nipple of resin.

—Once, with a cluster,
Faustus practised omnipotence
and summered a prince's vagary—

And in Málaga, now:
how the brine in the sugarlump
hones through the crystal!
How the shape
of a vinous horizon
remembers the Saracen!

—The pip and the tendril
repeating the star
and the talon—

The grape's mash
spoke to the tooth like a language:

First peach; then
the pomegranate's bitterness, where
the tongue takes the underskin's
tension—imagined a moment—
and gone in a comfit of melons.

4. *A Painted Fan: Seville*

The fan opens its decimals
twelve ways on a pin
over Euclid's spectrum,
a half-arc marking the infinitesimal
bound where the invisible
segments begin.

And from the round
of the under-arc arises
the hand, as the sticks smile
open, like an eyelash
on its iris,
or a plectrum
on its string.

In the painter's field—
parchment and braid—a shepherdess

stilled in a spangled sierra: lace
on a whalebone pubis,
Mohammedan and motionless, until
an impulse under the fan
displaces the air of Seville
with a python's sound.

5. *Street Song: Málaga*
(Paseo del Limonar)

for José Montesinos

The schoolgirls, with lockets and fans,
wait in the tunneling laurel.
                                        Half-light
has freshened their innocent starches: the stripes
of armorial blouses, peacock-blue on the coifs, cold
tesselations, burnishes, the buttony glitter
of folds on a dreaming pubescence. . . .

Mirrors and lions:
                    a hand-organ. Water-boys.
Trams.
        The vendors are priming their water-jars,
soaking the wicker.

                              The schoolgirls delay in the shadow. . . .

But one,
under petticoats, halters, and linens,
has taken the hand-crank.
                                    Drawn to her toes,
she kindles a tune on the ratchets in a stipple of hammers
and water-jars:
                    "La Niña de Puerta Oscura"

Her apron explodes.

Diagonals,
slashings, the leap of the harlequin tiger
in a breaking of biases.
Denial
or surfeit has shaken her. There where the braid
has tightened the gourd of her skull, her forehead
is deathly. The phosphor forms, sexual,
in the damp of her hairline.

A tram and a tram and a tram.

A meeting of flintstones.

BATTLE PIECE

(Uccello's "Battaglia di San Romano")

1. *After Uccello*

I have fought that battle in heraldic panels
Bitten in leathers, in Uccello's image
Under the poising and the leveling lances
Crossing the visors and trumpets.

I have seen,
In a hedgehog's vigil, ceremonious slaughter:
Halberd on battle-mace, crossbows tight on their jesses
With a hawk's extension, the rider's face
Bowed to his horse's mane under favors and feathers,
His profile naked to hazard in a locust's weight of armor.

What the fighting portended,
Or how, in a spoiled light, that leaden
Discomfiture darkened our spear-points, the guidons
Failed on their silks, and the drum-skin's hoop grew tauter,
No one remembers.
The maps and the outriders
Gave us no notice. The champion,
Sighting his lance's length in an umber perspective,
Awaited some sunburst to blazon that burden of armor
And interpret the contest's directive.

Nothing responded.

2. *Another Part of the Field*

An unsuitable landscape, surely.

Commanded
And chosen at once; inhuman and intimate, fated,
Familiar:
the light of apocalypse
Forced through the smoke of a burning-glass,
Bitumen and nimbus together.
In the distance,
The hearth-beds of millet in a harrowed and featureless

Valley, the brand of the husbandman's furrow
Rose vertical.
Pomegranates reddened
The leafage—an eclipse's corona—yet the season
Was iron: a furnace's floor where no holocaust was:

And the time was Armageddon.

3. *Encounter*
The spur spins. The contender
Spins on the cinch's wheel of his saddle.

He measures necessity
With a pikestaff's haft, from his wish's circumference
To the center of violence.
Fatality flows
Down his pikestaff's length
To the curve of his bannerol. He touches the barb
To his pulses, steadies
The shaft on a corselet of nerves.
And is ready.

While that antagonist
On the belled Arabian crop of his stallion,
In a turban's swathe, his lance
On the pin of his elbow like the hub of a compass,
Forces mortality's sweat-drop.

The spur spins, the contender
Spins on the dial of his saddle:

And the contest begins.

4. *A Reading of Entrails*
When the omens were served we withdrew
To a higher position.

We prepared for the reading of entrails.

We saw that the mottoes were struck
On a grave-keeper's cradlesong. The champion's
Shock on the champion, the decorum of armies,
The breaching of metal and adamant, breastplate and barbican,
Were one to the sybil.
The portent that orders all circumstance
Descends on a bloodbath, and legend is changed into chance.

But a legend was served.
Whatever the omens portended
Or the weapon sought to refine to its satisfaction—
The bowmen debouched in the appointed valley,
The paladin's silks went up with the angry devices,
Emblem and icon yellowed the embroidered borders
Defender measured the field with the defended,
And all was ordered
As in a decoration by Uccello:

A foreground of horses:
turquoise and cinnamon shod
With a jeweler's crescent: the straining albino,
His contemplative chessman's head in his bridle's rosette
Calm in the contact of riders.
A navy of javelins
On the overturned horses—a carrousel's
Splintered rotations:
the field of the wilderness cinder
Fixed in its fated relations like an armorer's fable:
The House of the Rod and the Water-Bow, the Cresset, the Sheaf and the Gryphon
The cinquefoil thicket laced with a pollen of poppies

The dismounted anonymous god in the gold-leaf rubble—

And circling him there, on the broken lunette of his shield:
Three hares

and a greyhound pursuing
and the invisible thong of the snare.

5. *Festival of Anger*

One, with a trident, in the stable's
Ammoniac dung waits for the bluefly's epiphany; one
Turns from the watery burnish, the millennial
Barrow that honors a monster,
And enters a labyrinth; one, in a havoc of horses,
Harrows the world's rage with his lance's point
For a chapel, a chalice, the cannibal kiss of a brother.

Fighters in the blood, contenders
Antlered or garlanded, horned and necessitous ones—
Old changelings of the gorged heart of the toad
Who come by ways as desperate as this
To work in the breastbone and whiten the cicatrice:
However we sham or subvert the indifferent disaster
Or give the ungratified godhead of the scourge
The service of the sedulous offender,
Your angers are festive!

Yours but to touch
The tinder to the tinder, the inexpressive
Desert adamant that hardens its venom
In the forge of the cactus,
And has no thought of sacrilege or pardons,
Incense, oblations, or talismanic letters:

that breaks
The providential fountain from the stone
And looks like history, or hope, but takes
A moment's inadvertence for its own.

I would fight that battle after the battle,
Inward and naked, after the outward
Packs like a weaver's spindle or poises like a picture
Baroque with the ceremonious violence of the shuttle,

The pencil, or burin, the matched and extortionate word—
The battle of the monster and the mothers
That no contender wages for a legend
At a charmed lake's bottom:
                                        where nothing moves but the imagining
Begetter and the habitual figures of his quarrel—
Who sees, beyond the landscape of surrender,
The pomegranates redden in a pomp of laurel,
The furrow blazing like a revelation—
And circling him there, still placeless and disimagined,
Three hares
                  and a greyhound pursuing
                                      and the invisible thong of the snare.

LIVES OF MRS. GALE

1. *Death and the Next of Kin*

My pity followed your plaid back, into the sun, to the car
in a holocaust that would rattle you home
from the furniture oil and detergents and the splintering
telephone bell in the vacuum's hoses,
to your porch in South Shaftsbury.
                                                            There, by the cutouts of poodle
and duck in the flowering pig-dirt, the cast-iron cat on the maple
flashing its egg-yolk enamels, the denims and doilies,
Puss-in-Boots in a pinafore tinted in tripes and molasses
on tinfoil, Roy and his bottle—the Unthinkable struck.
The hairs of your head stood on end. And at last,
in the sweat of your glasses,
                                                              you wept.

2. *Death and the Seventh Son*

A seventh son, or a last—
however you reckoned it:

                                                          The boy in the bulldozer
never needing you less, the untender; the wayward
and quarrelsome father and unwitting
offender, out of love with the Law, straddling
a cloud with an aerial to pleasure
your Sundays; easy with tears,
                                                                like yourself . . .

On your way to the Hospital, with the face in the oxygen
bag coming closer, some things fell together:
Bertie and Isobel, runaways. The smashup
near White River. Sticks and a star
in a soldier's necropolis. Arthritical weather,
with the well-drillers gouging the gardens, and the water
at two hundred feet showing gritty—

                                                                                  no use to harden
the heart or take on!

If the answer was bitter—
something you'd done, something you'd found and forgotten, well
that was for later—the more was the pity!
But it all added up into *Cancer.*

3. *Death Watch*
In the wallpaper jungle, with the stove
snuffling lamp-oil and the living-room crammed with a death,
the question resumed.

The death of a son is momentous.
It gathers the glaze in linoleum
parlors, blues the laces with starches, hardens
the nooses of neckties and buttons up collars,
and waits for our love, like a service.

The Thing that was meant—
the face in the oval that looked toward the face in the casket
where the range of the Thinkable crashed on a death-date—

hostile alike to consent and forgiveness—
wanting only
denial—

a Vermonter would know how to choose between sugar
and granite.

And the death of a son needed granite.

4. *The Beast in the Quarry*
That quarry in Danby!

The blocks came out smoking
with spray and acetylene. The heft of a mountain, the electric
and diamond of drillers, the marks of its anger were on it.

One could picnic on granite. Cobble pathways. And in June,
in the melted abysses, where the terrible adamant mounted
or fell, out of birch into fire, one could dive toward the time of a planet.

It was marble—the negations of marble—that counted!

So you strove with that sleepy destroyer in the maw
of the quarry where a season lay locked in its guilty
mutations.
                    The spider-plant greened on the window.

The ground-thaw
worked on the slate in the pit of the well, a pillar
of drouth in the garden, the cats, and the crosses.

Denial and pain were made perfect.

                                        And two summers later,
after the lawyers and losses,
the water came up!
                                It rose three hundred feet
in the main, breaking strong in the pipe-elbows.
                                              For the first time
the tap in your kitchen ran
                                        hot and cold,
                                              your weariness bathed
to its length in a porcelain tub.

                                        And the taste of the water was sweet.

THE LIGHTNING-ROD MAN

for Howard Nemerov

1. *Calligrams*

Your Chinese poets in a jovial dynasty
would have ordered things otherwise:
                                                    two rhyming topers
sculling in lotus-pods in a casual dory,
stopped by a calligram:
                                        a scallop of water
on a carp's fin, with a brightening
fish-scale laid over, like a riddle in Mandarin—
frightening, perhaps, and premonitory,
saying: *Moon of ancestral Destroyer: think about drowning. . . .*

Or is it Melville: The Lightning-Rod Man in green glass
and copper, topped with three tines, like a hearth-god
in Pittsfield:
                        "Sir, have you ever been *struck?*
There are no castles in thunderstorms. Mine is the only
true rod. A dollar a foot. Proceed with precaution, Avoid
pine trees and lonely Kentuckians, steel sashes and bell-pulls.

            Your man
is a proper conductor. The lightning goes into and out of a man—
but a tree is peeled clean, like a pineapple.
                                                                Don't push
your luck."

2. *A Look at Lightning*

The bolt, taking the line of the poplar
in the shirkshire,* slammed past the bark
through runneling leaves, found an angle of shingle
and smashed through the clothes-closet. The desk-lamp went dark.

And *worked* in that room: a methodical killer
smelling of flint and burnt almond, cotton-gloved

*A wind of exceptional violence, often followed by rain. Regional: Bennington Valley, Vermont.

like a safe-cracker, cutting wires, picking tumblers,
moving over my letters, the things I had hoarded or loved:

Old pesos. Indian pennies. Loose change
in a jar from Gibraltar. Postcards from Pompei in unplaceable
reds: a cosmetic of garlands and winged *amorini*
in blood-rust and ashes, to prefigure the strange
and erotic where the bolt worked before. Still tracking copper,
it rode in the wiring like punk, exploded in plaster and rubble,
blackened a voice in the radio tube on its way to a fortunate
answer, and spelled out in Nineveh: *trouble!*

3. *Second Lightning*
Ah, but that other time!
The forecasts, the starlings
that fly in the pulp of the weather-maps,
were bland, to the zenith.
Cruciform in a garden,
I lay in the sunbather's negative world, in the dark
of my glasses, in the dream of a camera's
reversals:
blackest of all at the sun,
black where the light turns on hipbone and haunches,
black to the pit of the eyeball, where a feather of shadow
shuts out the stun and the brilliance.

Something struck
through the terrible gases, a fasces of flames
in a fist, at my brain and my blood and my sex,
rode through the locks of the Orphanage door
where my childhood looked up from the salt and the clocks
of a playground, a drill-field, a courtyard, noon milk
in a cup, a graveyard of cots, a latrine.
The thunder began, the unplaceable red in the green,
I saw the tines blaze on the head of the Lightning-Rod Man:
and I ran—

toward the Drum-Room, the Drummer, his man's hands
on my hands on the drumsticks, guiding the sticks on the skins
while the thunder rose out of the hides to the window-bars
holding the midsummer.
A gutter-bird sang in the tar
by the swings and the seesaws.

The driveway spun
with its institutional flowers, its identical
pikestaff cage and its cinder-track—
toward
my father, smashing clothes in a pressing machine, a daguerreotype
face looking back over ashes and the leonine
threads in the scrolls
—dead and intent on his dying—
matching the seam of a trouser-leg over the seam, locking the sections,
applying the steam and the paddle

while the mica and iodine fell.

4. *View of Toledo*
What does the lightning intend?
The wish is beneficent, surely,
that bends toward such brightness to show us the shape of our terror,
or works in a cloud on a city's unpeopled perspectives—
not with the dark and the light of a sundial's gradations, but purely,
in pumice and hurricane, all at once, like a landscape of knives.

As once in Toledo:

a Greek, at a burial, coming nearer,
struck at the shroud of Count Orgaz, found the eschatological greens
in the rust of a cardinal's cape, the gold of the surplice's
threads—
rolled back the stone of his eyeballs
in the place of the skulls, and shewed us the bread of our lives.

MEMORIAL HOSPITAL: OUTPATIENT

for Dr. Oliver Durand

Leaving that cradle of bed-baths and bells
for the hurrying mothers who summon his childhood
on the helpless enamel, he passes the doorways
again: the sealed, with the masks and the gases,
where blood learns its intervals under a bubble
and the desperate climb their thermometers:
                                                            the doors set ajar
for the fear like a colorless smell
in the night-light; the ward-room's window-glass cages
and graves where terror lives openly:
the aged in abbatoirs
with the ox's albuminous look; the arthritic,
alive in a fright-wig of hair by the turreted
bed-table, among juices and pepper-plants—
all that threshold of pathos exploding in chemical rages,
waxworks and madhouse—the paralytic's magnesium stare
and the plotted mutations where hazard ascends and descends.

He has watched with the murdered, a casual.
                                                                        Now
the corridors flow by incurable quarrels,
beneficent sponges, lenses, and dyes,
bearing him back across enemy lines
in a gutter of chloroform, where the innocent,
crouched in the cave of their skulls, on the torch of their spines,
celebrate their abstinence with animal cries.

He would say something, pointing his breath like an icicle,
shamed in his appetites, taking the knife of snow,
sleepy with certainty.

                                            But already
the shipwrecks sail out on their pillow-slips,
small in their bedsheets, unforgiving,
intent on the shoreline that sparkled like salt
in his fevers.

What would he know,
who returns with his hurt to the bran and the meat of living?

The mothers could gather him back to the night
of their laps and speak of his fault:
but the mothers are locked under needles and crystals. . . .

The car races its motor and guns down the driveway.
The pine smokes in its resins:
needles and crystals.

There is nowhere but light.

V

WILDERNESS STAIR

(1939–1954)

DANCE PIECE

. . . at the still point, there the dance is
—T. S. Eliot

The errand into the maze,
Emblem, the heel's blow upon space,
Speak of the need and order the dancer's will.
But the dance is still.

For a surmise of rest, over the flight of the dial,
Between shock of the fall, shock of repose,
The flesh in its time delivered itself to the trial,
And rose.

Suffrance: the lapse, the pause,
Were the will of the dance—
The movement-to-be, charmed from the shifts of the chance,
Intent on its cause.

And the terrible gift
Of the gaze, blind on its zenith, the wreath
Of the throat, the body's unwearied uplift,
Unmaking and making its death,

Were ripeness, and theme for return:
Were rest, in the durance of matter:
The sleep of the musing Begetter
And the poise in the urn.

homage to Martha Graham

DEPARTURES

These things that live on departure
Understand when you praise them.
—Rainer Maria Rilke

1. *Vermont Quarry*

The look was never summer's,
And, with an altering reason,
Nightly the maple sweetened the block at its root
And opened its chilly cisterns over pumice.
Rigors of quartz, in the delicate season,
Darkened the sheaf and emptied the apple-crystal;
And always the taste of the granite followed the taste of the fruit.

This was for the wrecked hillside to say;
For the plough, on its side in the leavening cloud
And the dazzle of stubble:
Time was the emery's, and moved, in the quarrier's way,
An inch in the vehement dark
Where spectrums ripened to trouble a knife-grinder's spark
And deepen an instant of marble.

2. *Trade Wind: Key West*

Estéban, in a musk rear room,
Turns at the blown pane and spans a clear cigar.

Beyond,
A splint of mummying tinder; scarabs, fans,
Rocking the palm-glare, leaf under leaf, like rain—

And *there! there!*
That diminishing gust!
A guise of sails, meridian air
Bluing the Mexican floor,
Dropping the bracken garland and the herb

On verdures
                portents
                                gargoyles of coral dust;

Toppling a gull at the sand's edge, an overturned basket of cane
That leans to the ripple
and settles to rest
. . . as before . . .

3. *Tourist and Turtle: Key West*

There where the ebb gives phosphor, and begins
Its tender overturn
A fathom's depth in shale,
Under the mica gardens and the fins—

A green sojourn—

The palm, the prism, keeping an alternate myth,
Serene returns
Under the sidelong quibble of the gull:

And turtle fables, iron over pith,
That worry a marble saddle through the trough,
And try the waterline,
And rinse a mariner nostril free—
and cough—
And strike a strenuous sweetness out of brine.

4. *The Sand Painters: New Mexico*

The thumb, for a summer's promise,
Leans to its shadow on the cloud-colored sand
And measures its wilderness crystal, to a line. . . .

The shadow deploys, and the cloud, and the catch of the singer,
Leaving the pure stroke after the considering hand,
Wise in an animal stealth, abstemious, fine:

The small-headed goddess . . . fasces of hemlock and arrows . . .
Miraculous sunwheel, bound in a bowcord strain . . .
The side-pointing buffalo eyes in a pumice of mirrors . . .

Returns. Recoils. The enormous web moves under.
The cloud sways westward, poising its pyramid stain.
The spinner ascends the loom of meridian,
While, through the sift of his finger,
A thong in the hourglass trembles from thunder to thunder
And empties a season of rain.

5. *Celebrated Jumping Frog: Calaveras County*

Gradation, gradation—then a sudden leap.
—André Gide

Bells in the valley where the sheep
Lean to the slope in the flawing snow;
And still the frogs of Calaveras keep
Athenian laughter in the quartz's sleep:
Sweetness of metal: balsam and alkali
Between the serpent's ages and the sea.

Only the human watcher waits, apart,
Smiling the blind denial of his woe—
Masquer and malcontent, bounded by a heart,
Lending the whittler's trifle of his art
To what the olive and the orange bless:
A pedant-in-a-basket, saying: *yes!*

While, with an ironist's consent,
A multiple summer flashes, from below,
The poppy and the pomegranate's intent—
Faggot of grapestock—and the leaf is bent:
And breaking from the buckshot and the bog,
The pledge is paid, that lost the jumping frog.

6. *Ditty: Moby Dick at Nantucket (1942)*
I saw, over the gun's bore this summer,
In a trick of light,

The young boats with a dazed sail
And finical spars spanned tight
To charm the inland comer
By the cropped wave with a child's guess of a whale—

And cheered, in a lucky charade,
For the white whale-hump and the Spearer,
Playing the innocent fraud
Of the Death of the Terror,
Till the sail drew nearer

And the fable went down
Under the waste dune
And the pat verge of the hedge,
And, out of the water's edge,
Rose, in the cold salt, the blue bore of the gun.

7. *Cactus Gardens: Oaxaca*

It is no common sun
That opens a collar of horn
And forces the thorn-point's ascension.
What is won
In the cactus's knot—
The bandolier's crescent of bullets, or the oval
That closes a god's meditation—
Strikes on the cactus's paddle
And shows, in a disk of sweat, the incendiary, salt angel.

Not that serener invention:
Our wayfarer's Lady, disclosed in a mountain cantina,
Poised upon trefoil, treading the fountains of tallow,
Her slipper's point grazing the altar-stone, haggard
With glass and perspective.

Not hers,
But the desert's intention:
The cactus's paddle

Unharmed in the holocaust, bone-white on tin:
The wilderness mercy reversed in a brazen arena
Scored with the cactus's fiber:
The fronds of unfailing maguey
That take the mirage of the world and burnish all distance to one:

This way, the sunburst of thorn, that way, the thorn-burst of sun.

8. *Bullring: Plaza Mexico*
In the funnel's baroque,
Where dark and light, like axeblades facing,
Mimicked the murderer's stroke:
The bull's double peak and the decimal spacing
Of twinned banderillas—*two and two and two*—
The yoke of magenta and maize on the holocaust's field; and below,
The breathing of Samson, in a cable of lather and spittle.

His death gave to the blackening ring
More than the hilt at rest in a column of gristle
Or the agonist's warlock shared in a multitude's shadow—
Gave fear, in the hump where the rapier rode, without anger,
Odor of milk and lament, the wafer and manger,
The cape's corolla and the ruining Spring

And Dionysus drowsing in a meadow.

9. *Near Iguala: Market*

"Is good, joven?"

The shadower bears
Wicker of sweet savor: the festival bread
And the orange's cusp on his head.

Early
The bandages rise over pestilent cobble

For the awning's asylum. Color will spread
In the trophy of ice,
The pomegranate bleed under leather;
And carnage's midday will gather
The worm on the tine of the skewer and the rind in the rubble.

But morning is ample. . . . Dynamite. Bells.
The tiles' ablution in a running of ocher and blood.
A dinting of blueness—
The hammer on silver—the stranger's mnemonic of smells.

A wire in the wood
Practises yesterday's tenderness.
                                                            Dewless,
The burro ascends in a garland of flies.
The cupola's noon is forever.

"Is good!"

10. *Valley of Virginia*

for Evelina O. Wiggins

The bird's round, begun
In dogwood's mortality, in the pit of the petal's serration,
Fails, to our hazard. Whatever the casuist sang
To lighten a planet's momentum or charm our mistrust—
The dogwood is edged with a fang
And prepares its corruptible property: a crescent of rust
In the terrible oxide of sun.

For praise's vocation,
What but the heart's whole charity? The dogwood
Fails, to our hazard, if color
Harden my brother's darkness, like a scar,
And trothless in midsummer's valor
The trout drives Noah's rainbow through the water
And mockingbird says: *daystar . . . daystar . . .*

11. *Cricket Hill: Vermont*

Place there is none: we go backward and forward, and there is no place.
—St. Augustine

The wish brought me, at last,
To country shingle under a panic cloud,
Where, from the field's edge, under my heart's dead weight,
Over the bells of fodder and the slate,
The steep rain struck and aerial tinders passed
And the harrow's crescent, bloody with idleness, showed.

There, the unsmiling providence of the year
Gathered the extravagant blazons of its loss:
The apple's defection, genius of vinegar,
Struck on the whirling fly; the spine and the stalk;
Axe-helve and trident; spoilure and overplus—
And rose in the horn and richened its husk; *and broke!*

And moved, in the cricket's interval of pause,
Bearing the blazing rondure of a season
Toward those enormous countries of the center
That open a side and bid the intruder enter,
Tilting a marble cusp to the horizon
And binding a doomed occasion to its cause.

And, in the wish's kingdom of completion,
Departure's placename beckoned toward no-place
And the expressive passion smiled upon its source:
The nude head yielded, ringed in its clear halation;
Prism and lash moved down; the kiss
Fell and grew great, struck, and was universe.

NIGHT PIECE

Rise, cleanly trust, divided star,
And spend that delicate fraud upon the night—
A lover's instance moving mindful air
To make its peace in dedicated light

Whose look is charnel. Lusters, intent and blind,
Give darkness downward with a glow like sheaves—
A gleaner's pittance withered in the bind
That keeps the summer godhead of the leaves

And bends tremendous evening under it,
Doubles its theft within a lonely course
Till eye and eye repeat the counterfeit
And shape the replenishing mercy at its source.

All else were ravage: a demon-gaze of terror:
The emblem blackened in the living head,
The eye, the image, and the image-bearer
Struck to an awe with smiling on the dead.

Therefore that bounty which, however false,
Tenders survival, and is purely given,
And lends the viewless prisms at its pulse
To make an easy legendry in heaven.

Restore that grace! Indeed, the look is grace
That deals this desert providence in air
And lifts a deathshead, burning, into place
To serve a lover's faith.
Rise, carrion star.

KARAMAZOV

1. *Smerdyakov with a Guitar*

Who doesn't wish his father dead?
—Ivan Karamazov

I looked from the stairwell.

The scream
Of the feigned fall whirred in my throat,
No longer dissembled, and my mother arose from the dung
Big with my outrage.
The cellar-door swung . . .

And I moved through an epilept's dream:
A guitar and a melon, floretted, a noose and a fang,
A cradle that pulsed like a heart and a crystal that sprang,
Showing my father asleep in his spilth in a streamer of gall,
His nakedness sparkling like alcohol . . .

And I lifted my birth, like a jawbone:
"Is it now, Mother?"
I called to the stairwell: *"Mother, do we tumble him now?"*

—The melon-rind tightened. The strings of the fingerboard trembled—

And: *"Murderer!"* came in the pause. *"Would you murder the Husbandman?
Bow!
Bow!"* said my mother: *"Bow down to the innocent cause!"*

So I beat on the rind with my jawbone
and bowed to my father

And sang.

2. *Alyosha's Funeral Service*

Instead of lenten oil, I will give you suckling pig and kasha.
—Karamazov

If the child's tooth
Fall on the unoffending finger, the finger
Bleeds for it, and the stone shows blood.

I am content with that.
It suffices for crucifixion.

It was corruption's smell that led me to my father,
A carrion way through the saint's phosphorescence
And the faulting mind of my brother, to the incorruptible Presence,
Where, at the horn's end, awaiting the idiot Bringer,
A child's death babbles of dogs in an innocent fiction
And all things acknowledge the dissolute beast of the good.

Construe, little pigeons:
How we squandered that ruin of fathers,
And how the inexhaustible fathers restore us!
Old liars, dividing the verities,
Broken-haired mountebanks, eaters of cabbage and gudgeon,
Snoring in spittle and driving their murders before us,
Gods of the pestle and mortar and priests of the bludgeon,
Touching their thighs in an augury, and looking like youth—

Where was an end to their love?

When our violence faltered,
They contrived the empowering outrage to bloody our knuckles
And accomplish their perfect destruction.
When we rose on the smoke of the sacrifice, vaunting our famine,
Fasted and absolute, crackling the crystals of salt,
They broke the abysses and showed us the bladders of salmon
Sowing the deluge like pollen.

Their benevolence altered
The zenith's unsparing progressions and the span of the sickle,
Calling the figures of dread and credulity up
And shaping the season's similitudes for the lover:

The thread of the mayflower, beforehand, stilting a cup
On the scrolled leaf and the imminent foils of summer;
The skunk in the shorn grass, in chicory and clover,
Forcing his whiteness under a ringing of stars;
The moth in a pathos of veins,
cadaver of perishing color . . .

In whatever defiled or affronted us—
The coveter's rage that we dreamed on the beds of our neighbors,
Crimes, contradictions, enigmas, anomalies, wars,
Chance's inspired alternations at play with the possible,
Perfidies, nightmares, vendettas—
they haunted us,
Demanding a parricide's justice to hallow their labors
And work the design of their voices.
Their gift was dismay and unreason: the saving enormity
That heeled on its instincts and bayed its intent, like a dog,
Grinding the gristle and bone of the spirit's deformity
And pursuing its will-to-perfection into the bog.

For their need was profane, like our own—

a dream of abundance
In the lewd cornucopia's helix that bounds the abyss
And whirls the extremes of our will on its blinding redundance:
The rout of the priest and the scribe and the epilept beggar,
Beads, lacerations, and martyrdoms—
Armageddons, gardens . . .
The equivocal vision of judgment concealed in a parable
Where the intriguer's coffin waits, and the intriguer,
Forever uninnocent, sways toward the terrible wardens,
While over the leveling rifles,
A rider approaches upon the inquisitor's errand,
Bearing the pardon that murders, and the murder that pardons.

THE HABIT OF ANGELS

1. *Jacob and His Angel*

I will not let thee go, except thou bless me.

Contest, the habit of angels,
Tempted the man from the wilderness stair.
He rose from his dream of the sheaves and the climbing evangels
And clasped his antagonist there.

And tasting his want in the ritual's enterprise,
He swayed on the blaze of that shoulder and emptied his strength
And saw (it may be) in the ring of the combatant's eyes
The ladder's verge, at length.

What sued for the blessing and humbled the angel's election
Was known to his brother: a carnival cheat of the shell,
A modern advantage that purchased an omen's perfection
And cozened the boy from the well,

And drew, in the chance of the pit, the guile of the dreamer,
The blood-clabbered god in the road backdrawn by the hair:
The bounty of Egypt, the thrift of the merchant-redeemer,
The void at the sheer of the stair.

2. *Lamentation of Job*

And he took himself a potsherd to scrape himself withal and he sat among the ashes.

Was it to startle the Adversary in His own element
That that good man opened the doorway of his flesh
And measured his body's rebellion with the tempter's intent,
In a figure of ash?

The havens of Shaddai, the oils of the assuager
Bled, with the ministering potsherd, for this man,
As again, in the cynical service of the wager,
The afflictions of Egypt began:

Ravage of children and the root's betrayal,
Marrow's infirmity and the sickening air,
Havoc and canker, murrain and massacre
And all the maniac rhetoric of denial.

But most, when the intellectual justice of the city
Darkened his loss with the grasshopper's counsel, and killed,
And spoke in the Comforter's comedy of pity
The hero's despair was fulfilled—

Who saw that the tempters were three, and their solace,
Adam's contagion in the ghost's beginning:
Defeat of awe, milleniums of cunning,
And the syllogist's malice.

And, in the place of the rock and the ladder where a godhead faded
And all the inheritors of Jesse slept,
He watched while a pustule gathered. . . . Almost, he was persuaded,
And therefore Job wept.

3. *Another Sorrowing Woman*

Woman, what have I to do with thee?

I have willed the event,
At length, and confront the violent shape,
And break, on the pyx of my lap,
In the old, paschal posture, the obscene Innocent.

The pure vocation of that younger rage—
Godhead, little with woe—
Must bend to the stone of my knees and take its wage
And measure that murderous anvil, for the blow—

And die, for a mourning animal
In a schoolboy's subterfuge of grief,
Taking the expedient kiss, the coronal
Maudlin with thorns, between the deaths of a thief.

Playfellow: go. It is the old exchange,
The Roman platitude;
And it shall leave you range
To puzzle, again, your pedant's idea of the good
In a child's solitude.

after Michelangelo's Pietà

4. *Goliath Stone*

Let all things that have breath praise the Lord.

What stayed, was the wish to praise
In a causeless occasion.

The wasp in the throughshine, by the unreal window,
Above scarabs, in the termite's detonation,
Snored on the blind glaze, brightened a shard,
And opened the hallowing summer of its pulses.

He saw the blessed hem close on the approaching sandal,
The bland linen scrolled with a double vector,
The fringe, the sponge,
The big hands in the harp's transparencies
Tensing the sling-stone, with the knuckles starred,
The lifeline pierced with the suppliant's fingernail—

The vexed head in its armory—

The nostril's volute in the beard's foil—

And under the crown's weight, the stone's three distances:
Absalom, Jonathan, Saul.

DESCENT IN A PARACHUTE

1.

Leant, in his fall, to question his confident haste.
And moaned. And fumbled the cord on his broken navel . . .

And rose on his arm in his fall, thinking ease,
As level under level,
In the brute and downward waste
(Crouched for the birthblow, chin to his knees),
He grappled his breast for the ring of the bone, in his rage,

And opened his brows, like a cage. . . .

2.

A little troughing the void,
Tensing its folds in the vehement interim,
Buoying its silks, itself for a moment buoyed—
Out sprang the parachute brain to recover him:

"For how, in an element
Of flight and fracture, reckon rest and stress?
Or mark the stroke and know it for descent
Among the cleaving zones of the abyss?

"Hurler and sleeper, who journey your self in your fall,
Time is a bowspan, space is a discus hurled:
You stand with the hurlers under the vault of the skull
And turn a considering surmise, like a world—

"And think to fall helpless, and turn on your arms in that dream,
Thinking the dream, chafing a word in sleep,
And rise on your arm to give the dream its name . . .
And tremble; and cannot break the dreamer's keep."

3.

And plunged *(keeping childbirth, knees to his breast)*
Beating his temples, parting a garland of bone:
A little flying the parachute heart as he passed—
A handsbreadth of cordage poised like a thought, over stone;

And bent in the circuits of narrow and wilderness air;
Sprang to the ring's verge, bursting its silks on the height;
Wheeled in the ravel; leant to the deepening blur—

As up, like explosion, the flint of the world struck his flight.

SOUNDSTAGE

(U.S. Signal Corps Photographic Center: 1945)

1.

Catwalk, backdrop, cable, girder, fly—
A schooner capsized.

Sea-fans of artifice
Buoyed in the middle currents; gelatin and foil;
Baskets of radiant cordage; geysers of frost;
Miraculous canvas in the glowing levels, glazed,
The backdrops weedy, like oil. . . .

The ropes plunge and are lost;
Are parted like hair,
Where, at the summit, among crucibles of light,
Equilibrist Gulliver
Calls to the carpenters in a tightwire vertigo,
At the Archimedean center of deception, unamazed.

And all that is, is film. Film is
The serpent in Eden garden, the cord in the chrysalis,
The bough in the dove's beak, trying the Deluge,
The thread in the labyrinth,
The Great Wall of China spanning the dynasties
Like a calligraphic symbol; meridians, staves
Between the upper and the nether icecaps; trajectory
Of shell and tracer-bullet, phosphor and satchel-charge;

The looped "l" given to the paper poorly on the burning tripod

And the victory over horror in an image.

2.

The boy in the uniform of Oberleutnant, the demoniac flyer,
Will not bleed humanly from the papier-mâché doorway.
The door
Will not close truly on the plausible flight,
With leisure for vanity, vacancy, mania, the stunned recognition.

And mocking the human wish for asylum,
Spray-gun and saw, the jaw of the plier,
Have outpaced fable.

It is divertissement, after all.
What is stilted in canvas, jailed to the plywood wall,
Stabbed to the floor
With wing-screws and metal angles,
Melts into vaudeville in a whirr of velocipedes
And a yelping of trained poodles,
A swindle of spangles.
Only the scaffold gives stress to the weightless interior
On the wrong side of the pattern: the artisan's touch of the actual.

3.

Yet teased out of thought,
The smiling divination of the Spool
Whirls forever in the large eye of Keats, heavy with film.
For even that Attic shape,
The bride of quietness brought to bed on the urn,
Was not more actual than this.

And, in equivocal distance,
Necessitous armies close, image and spectacle wait
And beat on the canvas door;
The fiction
Calls in the camera's crystal to existence,
Loud as myself—

in deed, in ghost—
And bleeds in Agamemnon's color,
And is articulate.

THE SPOOL

They splay at a bend of the road, rifles slung, the
shadows minimal, their hands tugging their slings by
the upper swivel to ease the routine of the march.
They have been moving since morning, and over each
has descended that singleness, mournful and
comatose, which is the mysterious gift of the march.
Their helmets shadow their eyes, their chinstraps
dangling. In the raddle of grasses their solitude
floats in a drift of identities, a common melancholy.

A captain enters the frame at the head of his
company. His face flashes. With his left hand he tilts
back his helmet, while with his right he draws the
length of an elbow across forehead and nose, his
stained armpits showing dark. A bracelet flashes
behind him. The column recedes, rifles close over the
canted belts, moving up, the packed backs vulnerable:

(Cut)

Late afternoon. In the half-light a handful of blazing
sticks, four infantrymen heating mess tins over an
eddy of smoke, a fifth on his hams, his eyes upcast
from the rim of his metal cup. Nearby a corporal
works a patch into the chamber of his rifle;
he repeats four syllables and smiles sleepily into
the camera. The camera moves to the bivouac area;
a group, their meat-cans close to their mouths,
spooning the compost, Chinese-fashion, and clowning
between mouthfuls. Very close. Their jaws,
lightly bearded, the necks in their jacket collars
strained in an easy horseplay, the Adam's apples
rapidly raised and released in the human exertion
of eating. In deep shadow, the light failing,
very close. A private tugs at his boot by the toe
and the round of the heel. Deliberately, he draws
the boot clear of his foot, sets it aside with deep
satisfaction, massages his instep over a maternal
thickness of socks. He bends toward the other foot,
camera-shy, a half smile breaking;

(Cut)

It is not yet possible to distinguish the forms
behind the camouflage netting. They move in the
central darkness of the gun, stacking shells and
bringing up powder charges. Only the bulk of the
howitzer is sure, the gun-barrel crossing the line
of the valley under the tented netting.
A village is burning in the valley. In the watery light,
smoke deepens over three hearthbeds of brightness.
A spire. A siding. A ladder of rooftops.
The gun fires. The picture trembles.

(Cut)

An iron darkening.
The hip of a tank darkens a frame,
foreshortened, the treads close to the lens,
a rushing of hammers, rings. The lens is cleared.
A cobbled street. A row of country-houses,
walled. A rosebush in the heavy light, blown
forward. Dust falls in the afterdraft,
a grain at a time. The camera is watchful.
A rifleman moves up the frame, his rifle at low port,
his shadow buffing the cobbles, crouched. He pauses
under the rosebush, his rifle hiked. A second figure
breaks through the frame, freezing between the
foreground and the far doorway. The man under
the rosetree sights carefully. The second man listens.
He raises his rifle, barrel backwards, and brings
the butt down heavily on the door-panels.
The rifle rebounds.
He measures a second blow, his teeth bared
slightly in a reflex of anxiety. His eye is large.
The butt-plate smashes over doorknob and lock,
the knocker flies upward once, the panel splinters
all at once. The man kicks the door open easily
with a booted foot. He listens, bent toward his
rifle-sights. He signals to the second man and enters
the doorway, stooped like a man entering a cave—

(Cut)

Brightness through trees. A damascene.
At the edge of a clearing, a parked jeep.
Two medical corpsmen lash litters to the jeep
engine a few hundred yards behind front lines.
The litter-poles enter the lens over the arch
of the engine. On the litter, a swathed head, a shock
of broken hair, motionless, a fall of blankets.
The stretcher-bearers vault lightly to their seats
and move off at a crawl.
Roadmarker: *Battalion Aid Station.* A corner of
charred wall, rubble, glass, timber. Legend: *Épicerie.*
The stretcher-bearers dismount.
The film is bad.
Presently a gloved hand in a surgeon's sheath,
holding a forceps. Briskly the hand moves over a
circlet of maimed flesh noosed in a bloody bandage.
A scalpel flashes between the living hand and the
human hurt, forcing the rind of the wound,
filling the frame. The camera submits, framing
the wound like a surgeon's retractor, its gaze
nerveless and saline. The gauzes blacken swiftly,
too heavy for the jaws of the forceps. . . .
The surgeon at full figure. A breeze finds the fold
of his tunic. In the distance the litter-bearers are
leaning for the litter-poles. His eyes hold the optical
center of the lens, unanswered. His mouth rejects
contemplation, not yet relaxed. His hands are void
in their glimmering cicatrix of rubber.

THE CASUALTY

for David Schubert

And have your answer out of your instinct's need
to render its terror tangible.

For howsoever shyly,
under the soldier's compulsion, with a human gaze,
puzzling disaster at a time when terror was usual,
you bent to the bullet a consented will—
you ripened volition with that other deed,
valor's improvisation, the unselving act,
to force an unspeakable image from the Maze.

Infantryman falling, falling always: your fall is forever.
Fall to your certainty, no longer compelled and alone,
yielding the gunstock to the compassionate image.
Turn from the bomb-burst by the powerless river
forfeit in crossfire, on inadmissive ground—
who have become that Host the night-march sought:
terror's unique enigma, the time-server's will,
the shield whereon Medusa's manifest gaze
glows like a boss and confronts its deliverer
in the bottomless pit and the beast's face of the wound.

VI
SCHOOL OF THE SOLDIER*

(1943)

All Act is Virtue.
—William Blake

*"School of the soldier" is defined as disciplinary drill in facings, marchings, and positions. It is synonymous with "close order drill." For a glossary of subheadings, see *The Soldier's Handbook* (U.S. Army).

AUTHOR'S NOTE

This is my "book about the War"—a little compilation of destructions written in company dayrooms and service clubs, on army cots, footlockers in barracks, and latrines, at lulls and intervals during my basic training in Camp Gordon, Georgia, between January and February of 1943. As an anti-poem on the subject of Being and Feigning, or Language and Action—the mobilization of an identity regarded as "expendable"—its inclusion in a collection that seeks to encompass a lifetime's vocation and account for its silences seems crucial. There is left only to say that the text, originally published as "prose fiction" in the *Quarterly Review of Literature* in 1949, included other subverted poems that, with time, disavowed their pretense at prose and passed into later collections, as songs of a self in search of its personal legend.

SCHOOL OF THE SOLDIER

I. THE BREAKING POINT

i. *Position of a Soldier*

We circle.
We circle and are left to stare at the shortorder
waitress the valentine of her back toward us.
We are loaded into guncolored trucks staggering our knees
and cradling our handbags to make place. We
are marched to barracks. Hun hoo hun hoo says the corporal.
My cot is seventh in a file of fifteen showing
a bare spring a roll of mattress a khaki swathe.
Across the room fifteen cots face us in duplicate.

A figure with a pillow across his face
and his arms folded is asleep in one. A uniformed
rookie looks at us intently as though he meant to tell us
something and goes on picking tabs from an OD blouse.
—All right you civilians says the corporal.—Remember
your bednumber and drop your handbags. Chow. *(Bed Number 72)*
—Is it all right if we wear our hats asks someone.

Our civilian shoes wetten.

* * *

Ahead a door flies open.
A flurry of traysounds cupsounds odors men's voices.
We inch toward the stairway. I lift and lower
my feet into the ooze of the snow. My hand finds the dripping
stairrail. I pass into the solid windowlight and then
beyond it. I am driven inside flattened against the wall.
I look over my coat collar into the corner.
(Where was you brought up? In a stable?)

* * *

The dazzle is goldcolored. A crowned girl smiles
toward her bosom. Many points of luster strike from a

gold center. They tremble without haste over the ranked
tables; strike and strike. I shake my head shove my hat off
crush it under my free elbow. The tables are filled
with uniforms hands heads. They extend uncountably
as far into the messhall as I can see. In the center
is the cafeteria table with a clutter of KPs sullenly
spooning out rations into rectangular messtins.
A ring of gooseliver a ring of bologna a cheeseslab coleslaw
a chocolate square a mug of bean soup. I turn away
toward the gold luster and step forward.—*This is*—
The plaguespot at the base of my neck has begun to thump
murderously. And I am at the serving tables. I take a tin
plate and follow the hand before me. The soupmug goes into
the larger hollow on the upper left. The hand in front of me
reverses its tray. I reverse mine. A ring of gooseliver
a ring of bologna a cheeseslab a chocolate square.
I try to remember: *"The bird that steels himself straight*
upward—" I find a table set my messtin down drag my
feet over the bench stuff my soaked hat between my knees
unbutton my rank topcoat reach for my fork. A trigger
suddenly springs at the base of my neck. An ache explodes
toward the crown of my head. Strikes and strikes. Gold.
A dazzle of gold. *"What is our innocence? And what our*
guilt? And whence is courage—" I try to remember.
I break my bread.

* * *

I see. It means
that we are always to be in lines. Our place is always to be
that place and it is there we must make our solitudes.
—Where you from, sojer? The wand of Aesculapius
on many shoulders in a burnish. The poised syringes a swab
on either arm startling. He grips a forearm for the needle.
—Know Charlie Reade from there? The needle nips hotly
into the flesh of my upper arm.—Who? straining to keep
attentive.—Fellow name of Charlie Reade. Another needle
peppers another arm a spray of thornpoints vaccination.—Who?

I say—Who? I lower my head to the whorl of the caduceus
on the fathering blouse: *the life spiral the vortex sunserpent*
the labyrinth—Crito, I owe a cock to Aesculapius. . . .
The medic grins.—Next! holding a fresh syringe to the light.
Behind my back I hear him ask the next fellow with an
identical inflection—Know Charlie Reade from there?

* * *

It is our nakedness that annihilates us. Light
strikes us in hundreds *the cap of Perseus* uniform.
Our nakedness touches in the long lines and we feel
our singlehood. Little by little we surrender our shyness
our curiosity our deflections into reverie our humiliation
our sex. We turn toward the poised needles and watch
the syringes lessen. We leave our civilian clothes
at last—mounds of tweed cotton denim wool corduroy
smoking damply. We descend into our nudity pass
through the crude warehouse counters and are transformed
into quantities: drawers 34 socks 11½ waist 34 neck 15½
armlength 32 shoes 10½. We stuff our legs into ribbed
woolen drawers we weave into our undershirts a vertical
sliderule is shot into place at the seam of our legs we step
into our soldierpants as into a masquerade. Shirts belts
field jackets ties handkerchiefs messgear are flung
down from the clothesbins. We are faced sideways we are
made to raise our arms to straddle our legs to work our toes
to raise and lower our heads to button and unbutton our
clothing to shift our weight and relax our abdominal muscles.
We mount a small platform set our footsoles into calibrated
molds press into our feet. We walk down into hightop GI
army shoes.—How do they feel?—Do they cramp at the toes?
—Do they pinch at the sides?—Plenty of room in the toe?
—Wiggle your right toe. We wiggle. Yes it seems all right.

* * *

The end of the line.
The woolen overseas cap is pushed off our heads. A

knitted cap like a schoolboy's with a shallow peak
is pushed over our eyes. A helmet liner is forced into
our hands. None of us wants to put it on.
We carry it below eyelevel, embarrassed.—Come on.
Come on. Over your woolen caps. And fasten your chinstraps.
We raise the shell lower it over our heads astonished
at its lightness. *None of us is known!*
We are plated in half a skull. The thought of our violence
has even set our jaws at the same angle and our eye sockets
are *blackened.*

* * *

We are not allowed to detach the pasteboard tags from our
OD's They infest our sleeves pockets shirttails collars
armpits shoulderflaps. They glare out from our trousercuffs
in many bright colors announcing our sizes and our rawness
to the camp at large. Even the newly inducted civilians
still in the topcoat and handbag phase smile at us
as we pass. Sympathetically we pick our neighbor's
tags and turn our backs as if to be deloused: for
rid of the tags we are *concealed* again our solitudes
may return. The insupportable thing is to live between
our separateness and our sameness consenting and compelled
with our tags marking the line of our dissolution and
freezing us there.

* * *

To cross the line! That is the beginning of repose
the promise of solitude the cocoon into which identity
can fold itself for the long sleep. Perhaps even volition
keeps its slight germ there like the grain of mustard
seed: but only across the line. We bear our tags
making and unmaking our lines in the damp snow
when an act of gentleness might set us free each
delousing the other leaving us entire in our place
of danger but colored like it and therefore defended
like the grouse or the partridge.

* * *

We are returned. We are let sleep.
The barracks flares into horseplay as lights go out
the obscenities of the schoolboy and the braggart
the tentative aggressions of the lonely whispers
of the docile and the exhausted the intoxicated
confidences of the shy who lower themselves into slumber
as into a conflagration. I clasp my hands at the nape
of my neck listen for the throbbing of the plaguespot
press my skull hard. The snoring has already begun
and the coughing wracked intent wished for shaking
the prone bodies in paroxysms visceral angers
like depth charges. Body after body thrashes under the
khaki comforters turns this way and breaks
its slumber as a rock is broken and is emptied out.

* * *

In the sergeant's room two voices take up the theme of
women out of a paltry modern cloud.—I like 'em
small and firm but solid a real handful I like to feel
them things right up on me.—I dunno. I don't care
for the type that's always throwin' it up to you. There's the
hard to get type and the type that's always throwin' it up
to you.—I dunno. I like 'em solid and firm and plenty to
grab on to and all those scrawny little chicks I dunno. The voices
retain their unvarying earnestness and plod toward
one another on a treadmill. There is nothing to communicate
no act of recognition. . . . Then suddenly from a corner
of the barracks a sharp cry: —*No I can't no I can't!*
and a bedspring crashes to.

* * *

My hair rises on my nape. *That was the cry of a sleeper*
a deep sleeper in the wilderness of his solitude. He
has waited in the long queues by the barbed tags he is

wrenched by his nakedness by the driving and the silenced
needles, the explosions of melancholy and shame. He
has crossed the line again he has touched the quick
of his solitude at last he is unconcealed in his danger:
but his anger is thrilling and in the holocaust
of his sleep his terror is his own his solitude indivisible.

* * *

We waken into parades pauses numbers assemblies
short marches long lapses questionings answerings. It
is 4:30 AM and dark. I think it is last night. I reach
for my GI shoes and stiffen sharply. The dead weight of
the stuffed dufflebag still lames my back and shoulders
and the ropecut of the dufflecord rocks regularly
under my right shoulderbone. I look at the bulging duffle
at the head of my bed *(Bed No. 72 Bed No. 72 Bed No. 72)*
and close my eyes with hatred. I gather my toilet kit
towel set a fresh blade into my razor and clomp
downstairs into the yeasty latrine.

* * *

All the mirrors are hazed.
Cigarette smoke sways under the lightbulbs. Razors
combs towels lotions dentifrices jam the sink ledges.
There is a sound of water slapping into washbowls
cutting over enamel cement wood gargling
into drains and pipeholes a chatter like a brisk fatsizzle
over everything. Men in drawers towels shirts angle
seriously under the naked bulbs driving lathers
and razors over their faces. Others sprawl
on the six open toiletbowls an elbow on the bulking
tissue heads cupped in their palm a cigarette
smoking at the fork of their thighs meditative or garrulous.
Bellies are stricken in the showerroom and pellets
chatter from the snarl of pipestems and tin showerpods.
The gasp of waste

laboring into the drains is continuous
and everywhere rises that working smell of sweat
flat brackish proteinous rank carrying off dead
cells and hairs and leaving the cleansed flesh ready for clothing.

* * *

As a slide is shot into place. I eat again.
A slide is shot into place. Outside in a light
snowfall. A slide is shot into place. A slide
is shot into place—

* * *

Two metal tags on a tape doublelooped
lifted from a manila envelope scooped over my head:
BEN BELITT 31252939. I stare into the metal mandala
as into a mirror. It is I. One day later
a train is speeding through Virginia and a haruspex
explains: —Know what that notch in our dogtags is for?
Friend of mine in the air corps says they use it
to separate the wounded from the dead. Bein' you're
dead they prize your jaws open and fix it in your
teeth—like this—his teeth click on the metal
—so's the medics pass you by and the stretcherbearers
take the casualties behind lines. I have the taste
of metal on my tongue and irrationally I remind myself to try
the notch pinked with my name between my furtive
overbite. The tactile illusion is terribly real. There is
a green glare on a nightmare of naked teeth. A
slide is shot into place. A slide is shot into place.

* * *

I turn a pencil and face a questionnaire.
We are massed together elbow to elbow at little desks
like squared stools. At a given signal we will turn
the first leaf and indicate alternative answers

with soft black pencilstrokes. There are diagrams
to simulate patterns cut flat into pliable metal: flags
squares triangles rectangles dotted along the folding lines
and marked with letters of the alphabet. We are to say
where line AB would fall when the pattern is assembled properly.

* * *

I look hard at a diagram.
The diagram looks hard at me. I say the rectangle
would peak into a roof, the squares dovetail. The triangle
would ride into the peak of the sloped rectangle: CD
Figure would therefore be equivalent to line H Figure III.
Quod erat demonstrandum; Professor Luck ("Pot Luck") waddles
across the classroom on the raised clapboard platform
with his stammer and his pointer: 1928 tenderly. It is as though
the diagrams opened a door in Cabell Hall, showing
space, the geometer's serene. It is as though
the mirror gave to one's shoulder and one stepped into stasis
like Alice onto her chessboard. *I cross the line*
into a kind of peace, make my soft black pencilstrokes
as one would set foot alongside foot in a perspective
of colorless snow. A slide is shot into place. A slide—

* * *

We must close the folders now and pass them down the aisle.
A needle is jarred into a groove. A loudspeaker rasps
cackles soothes. We open our folders Test No. 2 Radio-Tele-
graphic Aptitudes two sound clusters small styptic dot
patterns dash patterns dotdash patterns. We are to
imagine which are identical pairs, which vary.
I shut my eyes to cram the drums of my ears.
Flap shapes triangles peaked roofforms float into place
tender their distances Test No. 1 *I cross the line.* A needle
ripples a spray of thornpoints vaccination *kitkat kat kitkat*
kit kitkit kat kitkat. Small clarities drop
from the amplifier onto a blind snowpanel.

A dance moves into my hearing.
I hallucinate. *Kit kitkat kat kitkitkit:* a music box
whose tune is time only interval without melody similitudes
"ghostlier demarcations keener sounds." I spin
on the hub pass under the riding needle driving my soft
black pencil over the dotted question forms
until the loudspeaker whistles sharply once and is silent.

* * *

It has darkened again. We have been marched out of barracks into the bare post theater. The corporal to whom we have been detailed is something of a parlor clown. He sees us a tristesse on the wooden church pews and would like to find cause for gaiety.—*O sole mio* he sings loudly to the first row of seats clasping his hands to one side of his chin with an exaggerated quaver. He leaps onto the stage desolated by its naked movie screen and two improvised card tables.—*The mockingbird is singing all the day.* The corporal turns a handspring and hikes his pants high on his hips.—Which of youse guys plays the piano? His tone is solicitous conspiratorial. He points with his finger like a squadleader to a soundly drubbed upright piano hugging stageright as though flung there. The benches rasp and settle. No answers.—Which of you birds sings or plays the banjo or has a mouthorgan on him? The corporal blows an arpeggio on his fingertips. There is no answer. The corporal seats himself frontstage his legs drawn under his hams.—Mean to say—incredulous—there's nobody in this whole outfit who can play the piano with one finger or sing in the choir or owns a mouthorgan? Silence.—Not even with one finger? Silence.—Not even like this? The corporal marches to the piano leans an arm on the upright crosses his legs pushes his garrison cap over his eyes and performs with an index finger: *I love coffee I love tea I love girls and the girls love me.* A stagger of laughter passes through the theater raggedly. The corporal comes down with a florid left forefinger: *My mother went to Germanee my father went to France*—Someone raises a hand in the rear.—There's a guy here can do tricks with a piece of string! The corporal pounces.—Whowhere? where's the magician? Up here on the stage on the double! There is a scuffle in the back and a nasal tenor twangs plaintively.—I'm the

magician Sarnge. But I ain't got no string on me now.
But the corporal has resources.—Is there a piece of string
in the house? he shouts into the funnel of his hands. He turns
to the magician.—Any special kind of string Houdini?—Nossir.
Any piece of string will serve the purpose.—Any piece of string
will do men reports the corporal.—You heard the magician. There
is no string of any description in the house. The corporal turns
toward the magician obsequiously.—How about a piece of thread?
Will that work? The magician shakes his head.—No Sergeant it's
got to be a piece of packagetwine.—Oh Sarnge! from a mimic on the
rear.—He's got some magic balls on him for a disappearing trick. The
insinuation is unmistakable. The corporal flings his arms out like a
target. A long sigh disappears into his bootsoles.—The jackpot!
Front and center sojer! The theater is suddenly black. A cone of
lightmotes granulates the screen and bursts into a moviecaption. A
marchingtune sputters out of a speeding amplifier and we settle our
bottoms for a Government Release on The Causes and Cure of Venereal Diseases.

* * *

ii. *Interior Guard Duty*

Remember the drowned parade field
frozen into whorls and ripples like a lake
floating a jigsaw square of tarpaper barracks and warehouses
the cut of the wind like a boxer's blow
as my guardmate and I turned in the Massachusetts tundra
on our tour of patrol
the dead weight of the riflebarrel
as though laid burning on the shoulderbone.

* * *

We are Post Number 8 and my guardmate and I
makes third relief. 2 to 4 P.M. 8 to 10 P.M. 2 to 4 A.M. 8 to 10 A.M.
with four-hour intervals of rest. We sleep in the guardhouse
removing only our boots helmets hoods and overcoats

with only the papershaded bulb over the sergeant's desk burning.
It is 2 A.M. The second relief have just stumbled into the barracks, warmth
sloping toward their cots like sleepwalkers
and breathing in the slumber of the sleepers like an opiate.
I see the latheworker directly across from me drop toward his bedspring
as though felled. Without a word he lifts his helmetshell
his headandshoulder hood his knitted woolen cap his
inner and outer gloves. His cartridgebelt drops in a furl
like a rind. He takes a comb from his overcoat pocket quietly
combs his oakcolored hair suddenly digs his knuckles into his eyes.
He flinches out of his coat and kneels to nick back the clasps
of his boots. They do not come off readily. He curses sleepily
without inflection. His head falls back on the smashed
pillow. He ceases to move at all.
The cone of slumber is heavy on his opened mouth.

* * *

I get up. I feel the scorch of the gunbarrel where neck and
shoulder join. The sergeant's lightbulb ripples out blackly.
My vision rocks. I lean for my boots, buckle them into place.
I writhe into my overcoat
stalled in the middle of the floor and watching
the papershaded bulb terracottacolored where the paper
almost touches the bulb. I put on
my peaked knitted cap my hood fasten the helmetstrap
under my chin. I put on inner gloves outer gloves. I clasp
my cartridgebelt over my overcoat and think of the cartridgepouches
stuffed with sham wooden slugs. I look for my guardmate.
He is ready at the door.

* * *

The corporal of the guard hurries us into a waiting truck.
Twelve posts in all each with its double patrol making
a detail of twenty-four. We rest our chins in our hands oddly at stool
bent forward as far as our belts coats boots helmets gloves
fatigue will permit. We lean for the shock. The truck is shaken

and we cut forward with a continuous trembling
as though driving against the grain. Post Number 4 dismounts
scarcely two minutes from the guardhouse Posts 5, 6, 10, 11, 3, 2, 1, 9
We are the last-post-but-one whatever our numeral. The
sentinels whom we are spelling surrender their rifles from lamed hands
rise into the darkness of the truck and leave a goodhumored
jibe behind them: —Take it easy suckers. This one's a killer.

* * *

Remember my guardmate's face in the intervals of light
in the jerrybuilt alleyways hooded to the lips
with only a spare strained nose and a cheekbone showing
heraldic like a mortuary knight. On the previous relief
he had talked easily and reflectively (good job
in a Massachusetts machine shop) boasted of his skill
with "anything that turned a wheel" of his preference
for the air corps in some branch of specialized groundcrew work
of a large family house and eleven brothers and sisters (—None
of us was cripples. We was always havin' parties and social
good times) of an older brother in Washington and a younger brother
in Texas of his dislike for guns needles knives. He said
he could stand anything except those needles and turned
the full weight of his unembarrassed anxiety
and revulsion toward me with a direct look as he said so.

* * *

Towards three o'clock in the morning he began to limp
noticeably and on successive rounds stopped to press
the full weight of his body against the iceplated alleywall
his rifle still leant on his collarbone.—It's my back
he said drawn to his height motionless. The winy pilotlight
on the firebox nearby struck the flaps on his tightened nose
the triangle of a Protestant cheekbone the patina
of the wall under which the seams of cut stones seemed
slightly magnified. Then he hewed
himself from the stone again and resumed his march.

* * *

But his pain did not touch me though I watched him intently
from the singularity of my suffering and conceded
the reality of his own. We touched nowhere found no community
of compassion in which what was simple in our wretchedness
could be borne with our double weight. His pain
had turned him solitary again as though its newness and intensity
frightened him and he wished to render it knowable to himself.
An iron ring of concentration shut him in and shut me out.
He memorized his suffering.
I could see him touch the quick of his pain for its shattering
replies as one tries a smarting tooth. It was then
that he dropped his rifle to the ground "against regulations"
or strained erect against the freeze of the wall.

* * *

Let me remember how I found the center of my pain
and struck him out. The advantage was mine
because the medium was mine in the same way that "whatever
turned a wheel" was his, and the source of his pride and volition
equally. His pain was *imposed* upon him, however: by the chance
of a gun's added weight by the musical-comedy loop
of the rubbishy cartridgebelt helmet boots and all the masquerade
of vigilance and aggression by the sham orders and the sham guard
and the converging exhaustions of the previous day's ordeal.
He was compelled to accept his pain *as he found it*
to accept it *anyhow* like an order of the day without
disturbing its accidentality even by a fractional part to bend
before it as an irreducible absolute instead of a monstrosity
or a cheat. It was this belief in the reality of his suffering
which rendered him helpless lonely preoccupied inimical
which converted even the healer's hypodermic syringe into a mystery
as total in its terror as the idea of annihilation itself.

* * *

Within my ring however all was known all was yet possible
even the repudiation of pain itself. Pain was there
to be seized and bent back in the vise of an elbow
or dragged by the hair as a drowner is dragged but it was not
a fixity or an incubus. The riflestock in my fingers
the blaze of my shoulderbones the jets of blindness and exhaustion
that burst again and again in the bowl of my skull the trickle
of blood at one nostril in the unendurable last half hour
of the watch the traction and rebellion of muscle after muscle
refusing to touch the breakingpoint in another step forward—
these were my own creatures in a menagerie of durance
and sensation in which I performed as ringmaster. Here
suffering was not a mandate but the beginning of perception
only, a threshold to be crossed into untried creativity at once
the breakingpoint of the actual and the vanishingpoint of the imagined.

* * *

For where is the terrible point of our breakage and what is broken?
If it is our wills that break then our exile and deception must be
unspeakable and our pledge must be: *never to cross the line.* But if
our wills must be created again and again as the great angels of our
myths have descended to us again and again then only the point of our
breakage shall reveal them to us as the exploding coal
reveals the intensity which created it, the organizing angel
of combustion. For the reality is not pain or fear or the violence
of guilty men but volition—the grain of mustardseed that falls
to earth endlessly and inexhaustibly and finds its flower in the
rubble of the adventitious. In a light morning snowfall my guardmate
and I walk the sham patrols with the sham cartridgebelt and the ob-
solescent rifle, each within his ring of suffering, inaccessible. In
the maze we circle and circle deploying about the breakingpoint
searching our violence like the beast in a myth trying our suffering
over and over to divide accident sensation contingency despair—the
tedious cheat of the actual—from all that is genuinely willed and
germinal.

* * *

For what is compelled is soon to be willed. Nor can there be any stay of our violence until our wills are known since it is in the waste of our wills that our violence begins and our innocence and our guilt.

2. THE VANISHING POINT

> *The greatest of minds, put on the barracks-square, will, inside a week, have learnt to move at the double at the sound of the sergeant-major's voice: (and) a lieutenant and eight men suffice to arrest any parliament of orators in the world.*
>
> —Robert Musil

i. *Close Order Drill*

The word: *to be.*

* * *

The lieutenant's lank form like a portable tentpole in three collapsible sections held upright by three metal rings. "The way I figger it, men, soldierin' and religion is both exactly like." We are "at rest" in an edging morning wind and the lieutenant sweeps his eyes to the ground in a tolerant grimace: yet his inflection is not speculative. "Soldierin' will take care of a man in this life and religion will take care of him in the next. The rest is trimmin'." The lieutenant walks a few paces, his fingers linked behind his back loosely. "Do unto others as you would be done to," he says suddenly. "They ain't nothin' you're likely to run up against in soldierin' that that sentiment won't cover. I don't care whether it's a firefight or close order drill out here on the paradeground or passin' chow down the line in messhall or helpin' a buddy when he's flat broke a week after payday." We chuckle reminiscently. "In the army it's one for all and all for one—everybody exactly alike, thinkin' as one man and thinkin' the same thought. Not 50,000 individoolisms thinking 50,000 thoughts." The lieutenant tugs at a glove and sums up—"*Now! When I say, 'By the right flank—march!'* I mean by the right flank and not by the left flank or the middle flank or the hind flank. I expect every right foot in this platoon to strike the ground *as one* and I expect—mind you, I don't request!—every left foot to make that pivot to the right together, in the *i*-dentical split second, on the count, in unison, as one man—not as 48 separate inividoolisms."

He calls us to attention. School of the soldier is resumed.

* * *

What fascinates, what mesmerizes, is the way in which action disengages itself from the *verbal* and becomes the *total* thing.

All but the artist are deceived.

* * *

To the soldier on the march, *place* is the nape of the neck behind which he marches. The point at which the platoon in "close order" is single in motion, as any good line-sergeant will confirm, is the point at which, for all the forward movement, there is a queasy illusion of treading water—of getting nowhere, simply. Time is dissolved in the formula of the march—rendered expressionless, collective, void, as in ritual dances. The Right Foot strikes the ground "as one" always, as the lieutenant assured us that it would, the Left Foot makes the pivot to the right "together, in the identical split second, on the count, in unison, as one man"—and in that singlehood, space and time humanely considered, the individual soldier, are annihilated. All are "as one" in a ceremonial characterlessness, a lunatic void, of Pure Act: the breaking point is exchanged for the vanishing point.

* * *

Is the individual act of violence also to be felt, I wonder—not singly like the act of the murderer or even conspiratorially like the act of the assassin? That the squeezing of a trigger is so simply accomplished and the consequence so inexhaustible, is in itself not to be penetrated. It is the mind which must defer and find the lunacy to render the action bearable. Even the real bullet must "tread water" in a demotivated void without reverberation or emphasis or ethical context, like an idiot's—a formal madness of Pure Act shared again and again like the body of a primitive mystery with the Clan.

* * *

That time when we all failed to wait for the necessary "command of execution" before coming to a halt during parade: the entire platoon miscalculated. To everyone's astonishment the captain—a knowing, soldierly, cynical man—swept his fists high over his head and brought them down on his raised knee as though snapping a shingle, in a child's tantrum. "Goddammit, men!" he roared. "Wait for the command of execution! You can't run around here stopping and starting whenever you damn well please like I was out here giving orders for my own health! Just because I happen to begin *'Platoooon—!'* is no sign I'm gonna order 'Platoon—*halt!*' "

* * *

My guess is that the captain's rage was not the result of a perfectionist's exasperation with flaws of performance. The captain insists on a full stint of work from every enlisted man—but he also has the veteran's essentially comic sense of soldiering, particularly when handling recruits. His belief in Experience's Dear School postulates our flaws in advance. His very tolerance of us is in essence an affectionate contempt. What offended him was a threat implicit in our misstep that rocked his whole soldierly fiction, making unreal again the basis of his self-esteem, his goodwill, his action-centered concept of purpose and reality. Where a *single* misstep would have passed without comment, the accident of our *simultaneous* error was, for the moment, an insurrection which rendered his discipline useless. We had violated our characterlessness. The underworld of humane personal choice was once more exposed, at play with Possibility, with its impertinent and tender insistence upon *creation*. Violence was no longer immunized by tribal ceremony. There was place again for the speculative conscience, the personal sin: the Act

was returned to the shifting universe of the Agent. The games of improvisation,
the rainbowings of insouciant chance working the web like the light on
an oilslick made their feckless bids for contingency, laughing the
soldier's easy fatalism out of countenance.

* * *

COPY: COURT MARTIAL BULLETIN PLEASE POST ON
COMPANY BULLETIN BOARD: *Specification:* Private R. L.
R——Jr. Company B 58th QMB
(laundry) did, at Fairgrounds, Nashville, Tennessee, on or about 18
November 1944, behave himself with disrespect toward captain Melvin
M. C——, his superior officer, by saying to him: "You aint
got no cause to talk to me like that, treat me like a man, slavery is
over," or words to that effect.

ii. *Facings, Marchings, and Positions*

A week ago our Littlest Corporal was setting his cap on his eye, hitching
and hiking his pants fighter-fashion, and plunging up and down the squad
line pursuing all the disciplines of the service. "You guy t'ink dis is
a joke!" he sputtered at indignant intervals, stopping dead in his tracks
with a look that promised annihilation. "You guys t'ink it's funny. You
keep fuckinaround like dis was nuttin but a joke!" His chin dropped into
his collarbone, plane, like a ventriloquist's doll. "But you wait! Just you wait!"

* * *

We are too much for him. Shoes are posted under bunks unlaced and gather
dust under the daily renewals of Dyanshine. An occasional blanket shows
a ripple down the barracks squadline: a tossed quarter would not rebound.
Hangers here and there are hung with the metal holders face *from* the
wall instead of *toward* it. A blouse goes unbuttoned at the throat. The

dash for sudpails and brooms after reveille has slackened off to a saunter. But the Corporal is subdued. He stubs his toe into the sand, passes a finger over the gold caps of his GI bridgework and turns his back on us. He has nothing to say to us. Phase the Last?

* * *

The sum is mercilessly clear: and in the outrageous comedy which we savor together the Corporal races with his cap on his eye, desperately saying: *"I am! I am!"* while his Squad makes the Pivot to the Right precisely as the captain would have had it—altogether, with its tremendous Left Foot, in the Identical Split Second, on the Count, in Unison—*and cancels him out!* This, and not our insubordination, is the "joke" which the Corporal misreads with the double indignation of one who cannot discover the point of the jest, but who nevertheless guesses it is at his expense.

* * *

I think of those tricks of reversal which, at a given distance and concentration, suddenly turn a pyramid on its point and show seven black cubes and six white where before there were six black and seven white. *The squad has come into its own.* It has flung the Corporal high into the air and come down on its own base. Nothing will now support it but its own weight and its own collective momentum. In the first weeks, I remember, our helplessness was such that we leant on the Corporal without discovering that he in turn was trying his own heft. We were the Corporal's first squad. The whetting-stone was as yet indistinguishable from the blade. None of us lived comfortably in our uniforms. They had committed us to a mode of being which we were compelled to *wear* without yet coming *to be.* Yet our uniforms *were* our skins and our only hope was to survive in the character of an instrument—a killing-tool bladed and hafted for the fist of an event which would in time make real our function. Either we were tools weapons objects—or imposters. Our search for our vocation and our self-esteem were one.

* * *

It was this that threw our dead weight on the Corporal in the first weeks, as on a whetting-stone. The Corporal, setting his cap over his eye in the nervy silence between the imminent maneuver and the command of execution in the morning drill, was our interlocutor. To him we brought our displaced *need-to-become,* an ungainly surrender of our persons and consent, and held them raggedly to the order of the Squadline. There, all numbers led to Four. We scissored the cadence together like swimmers in mid-channel, crossed over in schools and flotations like piranha, gave out an odor of nullity like civet and were volatilized in the pure encapsulation of the March. We *asked* that the Corporal set our heels together and touch our thumbs to our trouser-seams in the prescribed Position of a Soldier; that he enforce an interval precisely the length of an arm between one man's shoulder and another's, that he face us right, left, and about, "by the numbers" and wrench our eyes from the ground to the nape of the neck ahead of us. We asked, above all, that he keep the line *in motion* over the pitted drillfield until our diffidence and mistrust touched the cadence of the March and we were "as one."

* * *

What we could not foresee was the "reversal" that followed the triumph of our self-surrender, whirling the Squad suddenly on its own base, with its many lonely strengths brought plumb and positive with the real scene at last. Only in shocks, flashes, bursts of kinesthetic awareness when every heel touched and pivoted together and the colossal underbeat of the March arose unexpectedly like an earth force sweeping the soles of our feet from below and rolling on, could the truth be guessed. We, the Squad, the tools, the objects, were the whetting-stone and the Corporal was the blade. We gave shape as we took shape—indeed, we had whittled the Corporal away, until only the flash of his gold caps and his cry: *"I am! I am!"* remained.

* * *

The discipline that cannot renew itself is no discipline at all. The discipline of the drill paces up and down a small room, like an accused man in an antechamber.

Not that way!

iii. *Reconnaissance*

"I hear that some of you men has been gettin' into argaments with the southern boys on the question of the Civil War. It looks like the mountain boys is contendin' that the South come out first in that scrap and you boys is standin' by the Yankees." The lieutenant arranges an arm behind his back and grimaces into his free hand. "Now if *I* was to come on any two of you in an arg'ment over politics or religion I can tell you what I would do." The lieutenant links his fingers behind his back. "I'd damn well get up on my hind legs and find me a better place to set in. One of you is bound to be ig'-nant and the other a plain fool." His grin is acidulous. "Now, politics and religion is no fit subject for an active man to *argue* about. Take me, for example. You'd think it pretty silly, I can tell you, if I was to start arguin' up here about the Revolutionary War or the Boer War, God-knows-what-all-how-many-years-ago. Hell, why not begin with the Stone Age and work you up an arg'ment over who bashed whose brains out with the first stone hammer? That's child's stuff! It's not behavior befittin' a man or a soldier." The lieutenant zeroes in confidentially. "It's always been my philosophy that a man should look after a *man's* job to keep him busy and bother about the things that is really important—here, now, this very day. Make up your minds to it that *dis*putes over politics and religion has no place in a man's army as subjects for *argaments.* It's just so much water over the dam. When I was a child I spake as a child. They ain't the slightest jot or tittle of credit comin' to me because I voted Republican and Joe Blow over there voted Democrat or Socialist or Meth'dist or Seventh Day Adventist or anything else in God's good green earth you please to call it." The lieutenant's pleasure in the spaciness of his appeal to pure reason is apparent. "Give it just a moment's thought and you'll find that the only reason I find myself in one pew on Sunday morning and you in another (the lieutenant washes his grin with a gloved hand) is that I happen to be born in one cradle and you in another. Now, for Almighty sakes, men, let's not waste time on no such frivolousness as that! If you can't find enough to keep you busy, speak to me and

I'll figger some way to keep you out of mischief. And when the Lord's day is over and done with, hang up your religion and your politics along with your hymn book till Sunday comes round again."

We file out of the mess hall for a ten-minute break:

* * *

"You freeze to death at 30 degrees. At 40, by God you're froze."
"Find that football, Costello?"
"Got to ask the sergeant."
"How about a game of softball tomorrow?"
"Can't play ball on Sunday in Georgia."
"Jesuschristalmighty."
"What kind of lousy state is this?"
"Jesuschristalmighty."
"Was there an eight o'clock Mass this morning?"
"Nine. Nine for Catholics. Ten-thirty for Protestants."
"Uh."
"You goin', Costello?"
"Me? I'm a heathen by God and by Jesus!"
"Well, gents, excuse. Gotta shave, spit and shower."
"*Good* morning to you, Corporal!"
"Fawncy, ain't it?"

"Put your hand beneath my dress
There you'll find an ole crow's nest
Bye, bye blackbird. . . . "

"Army didn't do *you* any good!"
"You ain't just abirdturdin', sojer."
"Wished I had me somethin' to eat."
"Only time I ever get to town is for a good meal. What a hell-hole!"
"What's wrong with the service club? You can get a damn good steak at the service club."
"Yah! A dancefloor, a jukebox—and no lousy cunt."
"Always got his mind on somethin' to eat!"
"Yeah. Wolfburger!"

"Here it is five o'clock in the morning . . . lights all out . . . two guys at the machine guns, all set . . . Chris'ly blackout . . . Chris'ly Colonel was drunk—"

The stairway bangs.

"Where the hell you been?"

"Guard dooty, guard dooty! When do we eat? I been starved since yesterday evenin'. Better learn your general orders so's you'll know 'em, you guys."

"Hey Red! Hey, Red!"

"Let 'im sleep, you punk!"

"I look up here and I look up dere and I look and I look. And dere it is, all the time."

"Hey, Red! Hey there, Admiral!"

"A Catholic school is supported by the whole parish."

"What the fuck they want to run their own schools like that, anyway?"

"It comes out of their own pockets, don't it?"

"Yeah."

"The parish pays the bills, don't it?"

"Yeah, I guess so."

"Well then, it's their own goddamn business what they do."

"What the hell they wanna run their own schools for, that's what I'd like to know."

"You know somethin'? Sonofabitch cadre—we all stick together: 'Dress ri-i-i-ight—*dress!*' All time dressin'. A parade sojer. A lousy friggin' parade sojer!"

The sergeant hiccoughs, farts, hiccoughs.

"We was in the same calvary unit together. Look at his stripes, will you?"

The sergeant dives.

"Lay off, for Chrissake!"

The sergeant dives, for a direct hit. Whistle.

"Jesus, I'm rooined!"

"When you get that last shot fellows jump into a shower—a *cold* shower. Not a hot shower but a cold shower."

"No mail goin' out on Sunday. There will be no mail goin' out on Sunday. There will be no mail on Sunday. . . . Understand? No mail on Sunday—"

"Quit blowin' your top, corporal, and go out after that lousy mail!"

"I'm not kiddin'. I got hell this morning for takin' out company mail. There will be no mail goin' out on Sunday. There will be—"

"Know what I'm gonna to do after the war?"

"Yeah. Sell apples on the streetcorner."

"No crap. I'm gonna be an undertaker."

"Would you listen to the bugger talk! What you want screwin' around with dead people?"

"Christ, somebody's gotta bury 'em! Damn good money at it, too. I got an uncle runs a funeral parlor back home and I mean to tell you *that* bastard's in the money. There's courses in it, you know, like any other business."

" 'Join the army and learn a trade!' Whale-pee, sojer!"

"Yeah. The bottom of the ocean!"

"We're on an open pair."

"I'm on that pot. Give me some change, Frank, will you?"

"Two dimes, sojer. I'm short one."

"Seventy cents."

"Made a dollar. The way you guys crap out on your chips!"

"Wanna pair? This is a fast game, sojer."

"I bet twenty cents."

"Ace of diamonds."

"Seven."

Check. Check. Check. Check.

"I bet fifty cents."

"I bet a dollar. What the hell, who wants to be so miserable?"

"Spade."

"Pair of sixes."

"Holy Joe!"

"Ever been to Newfoundland, Mac? Got some islands up there. Call 'em the Mae West Islands . . . two mountains settin' straight up out of the water like a pair of knockers. . . . Ain't nothin' for it to get two below up there and they got what you call a horizontal snow—cut straight across the front of your face when the snow starts flyin' around the 15th of September. . . . *Catches* them two peaks on one side—the windward side—*like this!* (The fist is smacked suddenly into the left palm.) And one side is all white and the other black as a witch's tit!"

iv. *Scouting, Skirmish, and Personal Encounter*

In enemy territory both the hunter and the hunted have the countryside in common. The enemy position makes itself known to us only in proportion to our capacity to *move* within it and turn all its natural features into imagined relationships. The business of the scout is penetration. He loses himself in order to find himself, exposes himself to conceal himself, endangers himself in order to command the landscape of his security. He knows only as much as he dares move into. The point at which he ceases to move into the enmity about him is precisely the point at which the countryside is again delivered over to the enemy.

* * *

The scout leaves behind him all papers, equipment, and personal effects that might identify him before moving into enemy territory. He carries with him a mission committed to memory, his rifle, his compass, his flashlight, wirecutters, pencil and pad, and two or three clips of ammunition. He travels light—and *selflessly,* paying an invisible skein behind him, a death at a time, to the limit of the spool.

No personal histories!

* * *

In our night problems, too: that *discipline of silence!* The toe tries the earth before taking the full weight of the foot for the new step—on the forepart of the foot for the litter of twigs; on the heel, for the drying leaf. Canteen and riflestock are kept free of the metal beltbuckle. The sneeze is arrested by a pressure of the forefinger under the angle of the nostril and the upper lip. The cough is stifled at the Adam's apple. The command is whispered down the line with the breath partly expelled from the lungs and the lips to the ear of the listener. The man behind holds fast to the man in front, like a thread in a maze, and the Act is projected wordlessly and sightlessly into the unforeseeable. Only the leader may, from time to time, under the lightproof raincoat, open the catch of his flash and check his advance against the map of terrain. All is accomplished in darkness: a somnambulized reversion of consciousness in which only the factors of mobility and survival remain, and the annihilation of the drill field is complete.

* * *

Note on terrain: In deploying, the scout *becomes* the territory through which he is moving—indeed, he blackens his face with it before passing through it. He accepts the natural cover which it affords him—the densely leafed tree, the bundle of birdweed and wiregrass, the color of the soil on which he throws himself prone and "freezes"—in order to make possible those fine bursts in the open when even his shadow bears witness against him.

* * *

On the other hand, the error of the skirmisher is to cluster in groups of three and four, hugging the Squad instead of striking out alone. The pull of the Group draws soldier alongside soldier into a single place of cover and turns concealment into a target for enemy fire. Yet the enemy is trained to reserve his fire for *concentrations* of men and pass the single combatant by. . . . It is to be remembered that the inescapable, last permutation of warfare is *solitude,* and that from it proceed all the factors of the soldier's chance—his safety, his peril, his security, his concealment, his mobility, and the paralysis of his halts and his pauses. All is a convergence upon the image of the lonely combatant listening in the brush-clump: division and battalion and company and platoon and section and squad—into the clash of the solitary with the solitary, when one bayonet must waver and another must complete its thrust.

v. *Bayonet Practice*

Above all: beware of turning all into artist's disciplines:

Your disdain for accident, games of chance,
and the circumstantial—for action as a medium—
is perhaps equivalent to a contempt for life itself. It is
possible that your own medium, the force that works
the words, is in itself a hoax, and that the gambler,
to whom chance is a mode of *perfection,*
creates better than you do. Your disciplines
may be merely your way of fixing the wheel.

Why assume life will always come to rest in the cup
of your particular selfhood with each turn of the wheel?

The gambler knows better.

* * *

The order is "close" and the action "as one"
because the center toward which we are drawn is a vanishing one.
We "huddle" together, in Kenneth Burke's word, seeking
each other's sameness like persons overpowered
by the unknown. What we do not know
is the particularity of our guilt, the culpability
that is ours and not Adam's, and the extent
to which our violence affects it at all.
We think of expiation—
but it is possible that our violence and our guilt
have no bearing whatsoever upon one another:
that nothing atones. It is this that annihilates.
It is possible that we merely pursue the Act
with our hate and our love, warm it with our violence
and tenderness, call to it with our self-destruction.
The Act remains *ours,* and not *us* in the dumbshow
of the drillfield. Necessity has made it ours.

Nullity must make it us.

* * *

On the other hand: it may be that the affirmation of action
is indistinguishable from the affirmation of dying.

I do not forget, of course, that the will-to-die is an indispensable formula of the School of the Soldier. The tradename by which it has come to be invoked by the service is "expendability," but the psychology of expendability has so far gone unexamined. It is not a discontinuous *phase* in the subjective life of the soldier, enlisted and demobilized at will, like the strength of his shoulders, his skill in language and machines, or the adrenal good nature of his concessions to violence and survival. It is not used up in the stresses of the historical contingency, but compounds its consequences even in those areas not directly engaged in the expenditure. It demands nothing more nor less than a total crisis of identity.

* * *

I think I am losing all capacity to personalize sensation, except when, out of fatigue or in certain rare collapses of the psyche, I am overtaken by the action of tears. And even here, the cause is paltry or out of all proportion to the intensity of the melancholy which it compels. That time I smelled the grass and the salt sea together and was surprised into self-pity. That afternoon talking diffidently in the half-light of farewells and overseas duty. All accounts of wasteful, anonymous heroism and personal courage, the routine facts of dates and places, of birth, education, marriage, and burial in the newspaper accounts of service casualties.

* * *

What troubles me—remotely, like an explosion at a distance—is my numbness to language. I read nothing, write nothing, become impatient with processes of elucidation which are predominantly verbal. Poems exist for me in one plane only, and have lost their mobility and "legend." Nothing is multiple any longer, nothing *withheld.* All is brutalized into sensation and referred to a single determinant. I drill, I march, I exist in the present and I exist as action. I say: *to be.* I think: *or not to be.* I demand to expend myself in the action for which I have been prepared.

*   *   *

The Act! The Act!
In a fine ride of light, breaking powerful in a
topple of ocean again and again; again and again
the shore smashed into row after row of fountains!

Move into that free gift!

*   *   *

Autobiographer! Autobiographer!

Not to make *fiction* out of *being*. Not to make poems. Not to be singular.

*   *   *

Be. The word: *to be.*

VII

THE FIVE-FOLD MESH

(1930–1938)

Thou knowest this man's fall;
But thou knowest not his wrastling.
—Dorotheus

THIS FOUNTAINHEAD

1.

Content you with this mummied bread
Or ease your anguished fast with rain,
Lest grief, that sealed this fountainhead,
Yield you your tears to drink again.

From wells as salt as this, the crock
Can draw but gall for Laban's daughter.
Lay not your shoulder to this rock:
The bridegroom bends to bitter water.

2.

In heats that drew the freshet up
And moved in iron through the grove
A conscript and a burning cup
I keep: but not in love.

A harder dearth compels the word:
It will not merge in blood or wine,
But brims denial, like a gourd,
To pledge the bride in brine.

JOHN KEATS, SURGEON

No, no: go not to Lethe. . . .

Surely the level shine of steel
Honed to the littleness of hair
Is implement enough to deal
A stroke to lay the spirit bare?

The hurt lies not so recondite
As point may drive or lancet bore—
Yet, though the blade drink long or light,
The fever kindles as before.

However the providential hand
Hew the division deep enough.
The sutures, though they tremble, stand,
And cast the kindly unguent off.

An upstart's quackery, at best—
To mitigate the lesser ill
And leave, like an unriddled jest,
The ruined heartbeat ailing still!

Is there a stranger provender
To get the ravaged part its peace—
Wolfsbane? Aloe? Mandrake? Myrrh?

No, no: not these. . . .

CANTICLE FOR INNOCENT COMEDIANS

Keep innocency!
—Walter de la Mare

They smile in ceaseless manna-fall,
Flutes, and the quills of wings,
Who bear belief, like coronal,
And tender tokenings.
For these, an upstart whim has cast
The laughing paradigm
That binds the halves of first and last
To single troth, in time:

"Lay down thy brows, O malcontent,
The bright brunt and the dark:
Thou shalt be bent as light is bent
Beneath the burning arc.
We tend for thee abiding pledge
And drive in cleanly strength
The flaw that widens to the wedge
And shall be loosed, at length.

"The custom of thy disbelief
Upturns a double face:
She spends the massive guise of grief
In pittances of grace,
And serves a comic shibboleth
That puzzles as it goes:
'Elude the faith; yet the unfaith
Elects a winged close!'

"Itself itself shall cancel out
Till stock and stalk be seen
And doubt dissolve at last the doubt
When Lazarus has been;
And bring the mocker by the tents,
The mind of gothic mood,
To bind an old beatitude
In modern innocence."

THE FESTIVAL

In childhood, body wept to feel
The innocent anguish in the heel,
The impetus of blood and bone
To work some wonder of their own—
Some plaintive festival, intent
To burst its gorged integument:
To rise in rays, to spring ajar
In feathers pointed like a star.

Then, when spirit could not bear
The desperate season of the snare,
It dropped the indifferent body there.

Blindly, blindly, the diamond wheels
Spun that wonder in his heels:
The fans of flower-colored fire,
The crystal and the crystal wire;
The kindling tinders parted wide,
The prism splintered in his side,
Till preciously the blazing mesh
Leaped in a winged arch, through flesh—

Till, where the sinister wonder trod,
Falcon-footed, feather-shod,
Body found itself a god.

THE TRESPASSER

When last we came this pleasant way
The hedgerows blossomed, high and hard,
And blue with shade the violets lay
In every cherry-lightened yard.

Now, in commemorative rain,
I walk the quiet way alone,
And there are violets again
As blue as I have ever known.

Useless to barricade the flesh
To splendid branch and flower-row:
I see the cherry, flaked and fresh,
And smell the violet as I go

Perplexed past wetted flowerbed
And boxwood glimmering into leaf,
Companionless, disquieted,
And fearfully as any thief—

Smarting of some sacrilege
Too profligate to understand,
As one who disavows a pledge
And treads repudiated land.

DEATH AS BASILISK

O Deth, thou comest when I hadde thee leest in mynde!
—Everyman

The cold frond fell, looped to the leveler's foot,
And the horned shape labored through the flowery damp:
No tongue was sentry to the strange pursuit
Through the vaporous swamp.

A moment the brake shook in dividing air,
The massed leaf glinted out of violet brine:
Then, with an armory shock, the beast moved clear
Into wet and shine.

In bone and quartz, though preciously, the beast
Moved out of shadow, moved into light and wet:
The shorn fern fell in phosphor, where he ceased,
And rose in jet.

Like stone
on the charnel eye
the locked lid
turned. . . .

for Estes and Garland

CHARWOMAN

(Lower Manhattan—6:00 P.M.)

Clapping the door to, in the little light,
In the stair-fall's deepening plunge,
I see, in the slate dark, the lumped form, like a sponge,
Striking a rote erasure in the night—

And keep that figure, while a watery arc
Trembles and wanes in wetted tile, as if
It wrote all darkness down in hieroglyph
And spoke vendetta with a watermark.

That shadowy flare shall presently define
A scuffed and hazardous wrist, a ruined jaw
Packed into goiter like a pigeon's craw,
A bitten elbow webbed with a naphtha line—

While light shall lessen, blunting by brute degrees,
The world's waste scanted to a personal sin,
Till all is darkness where her brush has been
And blinds the blackening marble by her knees.

I mark what way the dropping shaft-light went;
It flung the day's drowned faces out, and fell
Hasped like a coffin down a darkening well:

And poise on the shaftway for my own descent.

MANY CRADLES

The soul remembering its loneliness
Shudders in many cradles.
—W. B. Yeats

1. *Early Testament*

The quieter god comes early to the childhood
That is unhappy. There is space
In that sufficient shadow for the clasped hand and the wetted face,
The sackcloth in the burdock and the briar,
The outcry of the renegade denier:

Call

To the strong child-god, for He has ears
To pleasure the simple hunger, and He hears
The passage of our desultory tears:

"My child, my child,
The feathers of my wings hang cool
And all your tears are beautiful. . . . "

He was my friend. I never turned from Him.

Oh, never say:

"At length he turned from Me,
Flinging the frank flower from his brow, leaping the pleasant stream,
Darkening the sweet water with his shadow.
For some implausible dream
He left the congenial hills, left the good meadow,
Sowing the scorpion through the innocent wheat,
Hurting with his feet
The small, immeasurable grass
That would not let him pass. . . . "

I had not stirred a limb
To turn from Him.
Most imperceptibly
I saw His vast loins girt and He was gone from me:

And so, when help was vain and He was very far,
Past the clasping of hands or the heart's call,
I hid my head
And wept for the betrayed, infatuate dead.

That is the truth and the whole truth and is all.

2. *The Unregenerate*

> *Escape for thy life; look not behind thee, neither stay thou in all the plain; escape to the mountain lest thou be consumed. And Lot said unto them; Oh, not so, my Lord.*

i.

Fleeing its childhood havens
And spent with fast,
The heart will beg its bread, at last,
At the beaks of ravens:
It asks no sign,
Invokes no grace but grief:
But grappling the angels of its disbelief,
Gluts its long hunger on the venomous weed
And the strengthless vine,
Treads the tart berry in the hollow sheaf,
And sucks repose according to its need.

ii.

It comes to me now more than ever purely:
How, fleeing the fabulous cities, one looked back
To see beyond the shafts of sulphurous rain,
The roofs of Sodom blazing red and black,
And shadowing the plain,
The hand of God laid over, like a stain.
        Where shall the flesh find sanctuary
        From the hard query
        That looks forever toward the burning city

And the mortal fault,
Probing the ashes of its wrath and pity,
Freezing the mind to salt?

How shall the hurt be healed, or the strayed restored?
Pity alone shall not restore the vision,
Nor wrath avail to thaw the inclement cell
Whose winter seals the fountains of decision
And stays the freshet from the unreplenished well.
Shall love suffice us, then,
Our elder overlord—
The mild messiah and the gentle shepherd
With crook and sword,
Folding the mole with the serpent, the raven with the wren,
The lamb with the leopard
And man with men?

iii.

Not so, not so, my Lord!

Cherish this disbelief
For final truth, although the end be grief.
Reject the willed pretense,
The vexed surmise, the wistful inference,
And reckon as you can
The gordian equation of the doubt
That struck the godhead out
And found no fruitful integer in man.

Now it were valor to unbend the flesh,
Burst the bright harness of dissembling sense,
The fine and fivefold mesh,
And loose the inward wound to bleed afresh.
Look for no respite of the ravening part,
Nor dream of quarter there:
Thriftless as time, prodigal as air,
Deep in the laboring heart
The wakeful blood, unbridled like a spring,

By devious streams is gathering
To spend its furious overflow again
Like fire, like foam, like equatorial rain. . . .

Let the heart accept this thing.
Confront it there.
The mind, though it delay, was long aware.

3. *Battery Park: High Noon*

i.
Suddenly the old fancy has me!

Suddenly,
Between flint and glitter, the leant leaf,
The formal blueness leaning over slate,
Struck into glass and plate,
The public tulips treading meridian glare
In bronze and whalebone by the statue-bases—
Elude the Battery square,
Turn with a southern gesture in remembered air
And claim a loved identity, like faces. . . .

ii.
Compute the season out of height and heat.
Cubes in the poised shaft dwindle. Tackle moves.
Descending diners paddle into grooves
And burst from bolts and belts upon the street.

Summer deploys upon the brims of hats—
Turns upon twill; affirms with colored drinks
A mimic solstice poised in flying inks
In Babylons of ribbons and cravats.

Here thoroughfares are blind upon the sea.
Enter the packed paths where the lanes converge

That drop the derelict straggler by the surge
Like targets in a shooting gallery.

In middle sleep, below the list of bells
That turn soft answers to a barge's brass,
These take their length in quarantines of grass
Among the pigeons and the peanut shells.

Their capbrims crush out day. Fulfillments leap
Sudden as bludgeons in a vacuum.
They answer to the pricking of a thumb
And serve him more than slumber, who would sleep—

A stricter sleep I guess, with double dread,
Who waken now and dream these sleepers dead:
And yet, these are my dream that dream the lie
And keep their sleep more deathfully than I.

Bend then to seaward. The element you ask
Rarer than sea is, wantoner than time.
You bear it on you strangely, like a mask,
And dream the sailing in a pantomime.

The element is blood. Tired voyager, turn.
The reckoning you take is yet to learn.
Somber, at fullest flood, the continents ride
And break their beaches in a sleeper's side.

iii.

Follow the loll of smoke, fallow over water,
The expense of power in retentive stone
Where the barge takes the ripple with an organ tone—
Over water, over roof, over catchpenny green,
Into time-to-come and what-has-been:

Into the chimney's well and the cistern's smother,
Resin and amber shed on divided flame:

Into the quick of the burning, combustion's vehement heart
Flying the summery floor,
Beating its pure pulse on the violet core—

Into the million year's flowering . . . the ageless green . . .
The sunken frond . . .
The charmed marine . . .
Time's incorruptible, biding, through char and pulp
The ceaseless diamond.

O lost and mythic scene,
Move yet within this frame!
This is that angel, whether gem or flower,
Leaven and gum and flint,
Recalled from carbon in explicit power,
Whose massive slumber wears the pure impress
Of old renewal and first fruitfulness,
Pledging the fern's shape in primordial tinder,
Sealing, in herb and mint,
The healing in the cinder.

Measure again the ruinous floor of the world
Beyond the park-path and the seaward paling,
The equal faces, stunned with light and void,
Tranced as in surmise, lost between myth and mood,
Derelict, decoyed,
In some astonished dream of sailing. . . .

THE ENEMY JOY

Tarry, delight, so seldom met.
—A. E. Housman

In jackal country, in the gum and umber,
That bird broke blank to the eyebeam.

She sprang

The feathery braid, the maze of slumber,
She trod the timeless humors, and the brief:
Her wings leapt thorny out of upper rain,
And chalked to stillness in that sparkling plane,
On derelict claws she sang.

What heart's-ease and what thinking angers?

Her wings drove black on bright:
For pure delight
The cold throat like a lessening spindle shook.
She sang the enemy joy as it were grief
And, with a condor look,
A summer's space in blue
Bore down the wreath like rue.